# Canada Curls

# Canada Curls

## THE ILLUSTRATED HISTORY OF CURLING IN CANADA

**DOUG MAXWELL**

foreword by The Honourable Sylvia Fedoruk, o.c., s.o.m.

whitecap

Edited by Kathy Evans
Proofread by Alexandra Wilson
Cover design by Roberta Batchelor
Interior design by Margaret Lee /bamboosilk.com

front cover photograph by Ryan McVay/gettyimages™
back cover photograph by Lawrence M. Saywer/gettyimages™
inset photos: (top) 1897 Central Canada Curling Association champions, photo by Pelton
C.C., National Archives of Canada, C-001340; (middle) Sandra Schmirler, photo by Michael
Burns; (bottom) (L-R) Dan Lemery, Don Westphal, Louis Biron and Pierrre Charette, photo
by Michael Burns.

Printed and bound in Canada

**National Library of Canada Cataloguing in Publication Data**
Maxwell, Douglas.
    Canada curls


    Includes bibliographical references and index.
    ISBN 1-55285-400-0


    1. Curling--Canada--History.  I. Title.
GV845.5.C3M39 2002        796.964'0971        C2002-910987-6

The publisher acknowledges the support of the Canada Council and the Cultural
Services Branch of the Government of British Columbia in making this publication
possible. We acknowledge the financial support of the Government of Canada through
the Book Publishing Industry Development Program for our publishing activities.

## TO ANNE

**The curling world continues to grow.**

*Between us, we have the joy of celebrating four other foursomes: Ward, Gordon, Janet, and Jamie, plus Deborah, Pat, Gary, and Karen; Jarret and Arlen, Emerson and Rhys, Sinead and Robert, Georgia and Charlotte.*

# Contents

# Foreword

**The sport of curling continues to grow in popularity thanks to the many major** championships that are held both on the national and international level. The presence of television cameras at these competitions has given more and more Canadians an opportunity to appreciate what the sport is all about.

The history of curling is as colourful as the game itself and it is timely to put together a comprehensive history of the sport in Canada. Doug Maxwell has done just that. The text is an easy read and the liberal sprinkling of photos and illustrations helps to bring Canada's curling past alive.

Doug is eminently qualified to have undertaken this overview of how the sport has evolved in Canada over the last 250 years. He was present as a radio reporter at the first National School Curling Championship in Quebec City in 1950 but his enthusiasm for all things curling didn't really take hold until the 1960 Lakehead Brier when he and Bill Good reported on Ernie Richardson's second Canadian title.

Some highlights of Doug's involvement in curling over the past forty-plus years show the various curling hats he has worn:

- promoter (Executive Director of the Air Canada Silver Broom from its start in 1968)
- innovator (introduced time clocks to the game; developed the McCain TSN Skins Game)

- builder (with three friends, started the Humber Highland Curling Club in suburban Toronto in 1961)
- broadcaster (CBC coverage of the unique ladies east-west playoff 1960 and the first Canadian Ladies Championship in 1961, and did the first live telecast of the Brier in 1962—the playoff game between Ernie Richardson and Hec Gervais)
- print journalist (editor of *The Curler* magazine in 1960s and for the past 20-plus years, the Peripatetic Publisher of the *Canadian Curling News*)
- author (*Curling*, with Ernie Richardson and Joyce McKee—an authoritative handbook of curling published by Thos. Allen Ltd. in 1962, and *The First Fifty*, a book of Brier anecdotes, with fellow curling writers, published in 1980)

I first met Doug in Oshawa in 1960 when I was a participant in the first Dominion Diamond D. We became friends when we met again in Ottawa in 1961 when he covered the first CLCA-sanctioned Diamond D. There have been many times where our paths have crossed since then, occasionally during the staging of a Macdonald Lassie (or Scott Tournament of Hearts) or a Brier, which gave us an opportunity to swap stories and trade the odd curling pin or two. During the 1960s, when I was a consulting editor for *The Curler* magazine we often collaborated on specific pins and stories about pins that were featured in my column "Pin Box".

I am delighted to have been asked to provide this foreword to an excellent book about the history of the sport of curling in Canada by Doug Maxwell, a curling legend in his own right and a gentleman, on and off the ice.

*The Honourable Sylvia Fedoruk, O.C., S.O.M.*
*(Lieutenant-Governor of Saskatchewan 1988–1994)*

# Acknowledgements

**A book such as this is the product of many years' association with the game of** curling, plus much reading and research, and swapping of tales, involving some wonderful curling friends, acquaintances and authorities. You might say it's taken me some fifty-plus years to write this book, during which time I have been involved in the sport in a variety of disguises. I have been privileged to visit most, not all, of the curling countries in the world. (That's why the column I have been writing for some twenty years now, in the *Canadian Curling News*, is titled the Peripatetic Publisher—though some prefer to call it the Peripathetic Publisher!)

I have reported on a wide variety of provincial, national, and international curling events (for radio, television, and print media), and I have propped up untold bars in countless curling clubs. Along the way I have absorbed a plethora of curling stories, reminiscences, explanations of why things were done the way they were done when they were done. It's been a merry ride.

First as a broadcaster (CBC and TSN), and later as a print journalist, I have been a witness (sometimes a lonely one) to the growth of the game over the past half-century. Oh, if only I had been smart enough to set down in carefully annotated notebooks the details, impressions, and yarns as they happened! But I wasn't, and I didn't. So I have had to rely on a sometimes faulty memory when it came time to actually write this book.

I did have some twenty years of files from my days as executive director of the Air Canada Silver Broom, and records gathered from forty years' (and counting) attendance at the Brier. I was there in 1960 and 1961 when the Dominion Diamond D was taking shape. Later I attended (sporadically) the Macdonald Lassie and the Scott Tournament of Hearts. I was a rookie radio reporter in 1950 in Quebec City, the first year of the Canadian School Championship, when I first met the legendary Ken Watson. There was also a stint when I acted as navigator for the O'Keefe Toronto Mixed Championship (during the fifties and sixties) including its move onto the national stage.

In 1962, the CBC sent me to Scotland to cover that new and growing event, the Scotch Cup, where I revelled in the lure and lore of the game and became enamoured of all things Scottish. All of this stood me in good stead when I was handed the opportunity to become involved in the Air Canada Silver Broom and the subsequent growth opportunities it presented.

I count it as much a privilege to have been involved in the development, and ongoing production, of the McCain TSN Skins Game, as I do the years I spent with the Ontario Curling Federation (now Curl Ontario). I probably should also mention attendance at four Olympics—but you get the picture.

Some of all this is bound to burrow itself into the subconscious, to be recalled at a later date, and then find itself in print. But even if memory does bring forth some of the stories, I would still need the help of an army of curlers and curling friends to smooth out the rough spots and to add details I might otherwise have missed. Or forgotten. Or never knew.

A small number of curlers were willing to read some or all of the manuscript and gently correct me when I erred, or chide me when I forgot something important. So I happily acknowledge the invaluable help provided by Bob Picken, Jim Waite, Sylvia Fedoruk, Linda Moore, Robin Wilson, and Chuck Hay.

I also want to pay tribute to my ever-helpful editor, Kathy Evans, as well as my unofficial (and indefatigable) editorial assistant, my wife Anne. The book is the richer for their efforts.

In my opinion, the photos and illustrations that are sprinkled liberally throughout the book help to bring the past of curling alive. While all the illustrations and photos have credit lines attached, there are a few for which I have been unable to discover the proper identification. Every reasonable effort has been made to obtain copyright clearance for all the illustrations, but if there are any errors or omissions, both Whitecap Books and I would be pleased to have them brought to our attention. In particular, I must mention the two Michael Burns, Senior and Junior, whose photographic abilities are world-famous.

There are many others who have helped in myriad ways, and I am happy to acknowledge their assistance. If I have missed anyone in the list that follows, it is not intentional. I readily admit I am in their debt. Nor should any of the book's shortcomings be ascribed to them: I'll take that responsibility.

Alphabetically, those curling friends include:

Bill Argan (Regina), John D. Arnup (Toronto), Bruce Bolton (David M. Stewart Museum and guardian of the history of the 78th Fraser Highlanders, Montreal), Michael Burns (Sr. & Jr., Toronto), Andrew Bruce, Earl of Elgin and Kincardine (Fife, Scotland), Jacqueline Campbell (Saskatchewan Sports Hall of Fame & Museum, Regina), Denny Charlebois (Ottawa), Bob Cowan (Scotland and Thailand), The Hon. Sylvia Fedoruk (Saskatoon), Doug Graham (Kingston), Nora Hague (McCord Museum and Notman Photo collection, Montreal), Warren Hansen (Vancouver), Chuck Hay (Perth, Scotland), Heather Helston (Manitoba Curling Hall of Fame and Museum, Winnipeg), Stan Houston (Bancroft), David Hull (Guelph), Clarence (Shorty) Jenkins (Trenton), Danny Lamoureux (CCA in Ottawa), Christine Little (New Brunswick Museum and Archives, Saint John), Jack Lynch (St. Bruno), Jack Matheson (Winnipeg), John McCrae (OCA in Pickering), Linda Moore (Curl BC in Vancouver), Rev. Fraser Muldrew

(Winnipeg), Francine Lahaie-Schreiner (National Archives of Canada, Ottawa), Emery Nelson (Fergus), Vera Pezer (Saskatoon), Bob Picken (Winnipeg), Rev. Wilfred Raths (Winnipeg), Vic Rauter (Toronto), Pat B. Reid (Toronto), Jim Runnett (Calgary Curling Hall of Fame), Rev. Guy Scholz (Calgary), Don Shaw (Markham), Ray Turnbull (Winnipeg), Jim Waite (St. Thomas), Keith Wendorf (Germany) and Benson Wincure (Winnipeg).

My thanks to you all.

# Canada's Curling Conceit

**The book you have in your hands is a product of the Canadian conceit about** curling. It is a conceit to which I plead guilty, as, I suspect, do most Canadians.

While we know we didn't invent the game, we know we have made it our own. We also think we know more about curling (we don't) and we think we are better at curling than anyone else (we aren't). And we are certain that curling belongs to us more than to anyone else (it doesn't). If that isn't conceit, what is?

It was this conceit at work that prompted me to outline a series of chapters for Whitecap Books in Vancouver when they called to ask my opinion about such a book. With a lifetime of curling involvement, I felt privileged to have been given an opportunity to tell Canada's curling story. There certainly was a need, for to my knowledge there has never been a book about the history of the game in Canada. Provincial and club books, yes. Scottish books, yes. But no Canadian book. Perhaps this one can be the start of a parade.

The opening chapter, I thought fondly (and with that conceit again) would be about the XIX Winter Olympics in Salt Lake City. It would be there, I told Whitecap Books (in 2001), where Canada would probably create curling history (in 2002) by winning two gold medals and prove our overwhelming superiority at the world level.

In my pre-2002 outline, I even suggested that the title of the opening chapter should be "Golden Days," in the certain knowledge that it would be prophetic. What a conceit! How wrong can you be?

So you can imagine my consternation, chagrin, whatever, when Canada's best and brightest teams—we can have no complaint about the squads we sent to Salt Lake City—stumbled on the way to the winner's dais. We came away with a silver and a bronze medal—surely an excellent result. But no gold. Not even one gold.

So, when I came to write that opening chapter, and considered my original title, a change was obviously in order. After a moment's thought, "Golden Daze" seemed more appropriate. But my central theme was still intact. The medals won in February 2002 were the perfect projection of the history of curling in Canada. The early days of the game in Canada, from 1760 on, led inevitably to those February moments at the 2002 Olympics. This book is about the times in between.

To say that Canada is curling's dominant country is trite, but true. For example, it's been stated so often in recent years that it is now taken as gospel that there are a million and a half curlers in Canada. But two questions arise: How can we be sure? and What's the definition of a curler? The estimate, because that's what it is, came originally from a survey that asked how often the person being surveyed curled: once a week, once a month, once a year. If you curled only once a year, you were lumped in with the enthusiast who curls once a week.

There is no point in asking the Canadian Curling Association, or one of Canada's eighteen provincial or territorial curling associations, or the twelve affiliated curling associations, or any of the other associations that don't fit either mold, how many curlers there are in Canada. They'll give you the same answer: "We're not sure." The correct answer to the query of how many curlers in Canada's over 1,200 clubs is: "plenty."

Fifty years ago it was estimated that there were 150,000 curlers in Canada, a number supposedly based on membership numbers submitted by clubs to their provincial associations. Both club and association knew those numbers were phony, but there was no way of proving it. How did they know the numbers were spurious? 'Twasn't hard to tell. Go to the club on any given night, and it was obvious there were at least twice as many curlers on the ice as were registered by the club. The reason for the subterfuge was simple. In the Dirty Thirties, and during the early days of the Dominion Curling Association, later to become the Canadian Curling Association, a curler, intent on playing in the Brier, had to be a registered club member. And since membership dues were based on the number of curlers declared by the club, most clubs found it simpler to register only those who wanted to play in the Brier or other similar competitions. So you had the example of major clubs in major curling centres saying, with a straight face, that they had 32 or 40 (certainly no more than 50) registered members, when everybody knew there were at least a couple of hundred of curlers at the club most nights. After all, 32 members with dues of ten cents each was a lot less expensive a club fee than with 200 members! But the associations realized that while membership numbers could be fudged, it's impossible to hide the numbers of sheets of ice at a club. So association dues were changed to an assessment based on the number of ice sheets a club had.

That's why it's a mug's game to try to state an exact number of curlers in Canada. One thing is certain, however: Canada has more curlers—way more—than the rest of the world combined. Put it another way, Canada, as one of 36 member countries in the World Curling Federation, has more curlers than the other 35 combined.

Another way to look at numbers is to consider the TV ratings of major curling events, which suggest that one or two million viewers tune in nightly to watch the major championships. It has been these televised games that has helped create the groundswell of interest in curling across the country—and not just among club members. Both the CBC and TSN can attest to their research that shows that many viewers are non-curlers who enjoy watching the game as much as the most ardent club shooters do. It's not hard to understand why. In some other major TV sports such as hockey, baseball, and golf, the principal object in the game—the puck or ball—is a small object travelling at roughly 100 km per hour. Even with the slow-motion camera, it can be hard to see. In curling the stone is much larger and travels at a much slower speed, making it easier to watch, and it's also easier to show close-ups of the action. There is time to explain the strategies at work, and the microphones worn by the players can help viewers understand some of the whys and wherefores. Also, the players themselves are not millionaire "hired hands" who move from one franchise to the next; rather, they're neighbours from down the street, or from the next farm, or fellow workers, to whom the viewer can relate.

The other reason for our conceit about the game—and we should be gloriously thankful for this—is that we think we understand the nature of the game, and its underlying philosophy, better than anyone else. We know as well as any just how chancy a game it is—"a slippery game" is the usual phrase—and we also know how important it is to play the game with honour, and fairness, and a respect for our opponents. I've tried to delve into the background of that important aspect of curling in chapter 5.

Whether they play it or not, many Canadians love the sport of curling. We love the sparkle and the famous names associated with the game. We love the challenges. We want others to know its allure and its joys.

I hope this history will help explain, in some small way, Canada's curling conceit.

## About the Illustrations

The photos, cartoons, and drawings in this book provide not only a pictorial history of curling, but also a history of the development of illustrations. First

there were paintings. Such paintings as those of the famed Grand Matches in Scotland provided an early depiction of curling.

When Louis Daguerre invented a process for putting an image onto a sensitized silver plate in 1839, he opened up the possibility of producing photos said to be worth a thousand words. In 1856, William Notman, like so many others of that time, emigrated from his Scottish home, intent on finding a new life in Canada. It wasn't long before he found his calling in a photographic studio in Montreal. Eventually a series of Notman Studios would stretch across the land, and his photographs would help illumine the history of Canada. Notman was skilled in both photography and painting, and the combination of his photographer's eye and artist's ability made him the prime illustrator of his day.

**Some ten years after Confederation, William Notman was asked to prepare a photograph for a Paris Exhibition. He chose as his subject "Curling on the St. Lawrence at Montreal," and in 1878, he painstakingly prepared this composite photograph. It was all done indoors, with out-of-focus lamb's wool as the snow, a polished sheet of zinc as the ice, and a painted backdrop of Montreal in the background. Sir John A. Macdonald is seated (with top hat) in the left foreground, and several of Montreal's most prominent citizens are also included in the crowd.**

*Notman Photographic Archives, McCord Museum of Canadian History, Montreal, #II-48781.*

To modern eyes, Notman's photos appear stilted, formal, posed. And so they were. The reasons for this are obvious: photography in the early days of curling was cumbersome, time-consuming, artificial. Notman's particular brand of genius, coupled with a painstaking effort, produced a social commentary that has enriched the McCord Museum at McGill University in Montreal, and helps to portray our past, including the sport of curling.

Getting one image onto a glass plate required the subject to remain absolutely still for 15 to 30 seconds, which meant that Notman (or any of his employee photographers) had to use props that could assist a subject to remain motionless. In addition, Notman used a variety of tricks to create photos that appealed to the public. Outdoor winter scenes were shot indoors, with sheep's wool (slightly out of focus) made to look like snow. Ice was, in reality, a sheet of highly polished zinc. Night scenes were illumined with magnesium flares. Falling snow was white paint sprayed into the air, and caught, as it fell, on a glass plate.

**Miss V. Allen poses for a curling composite photo at the Notman Studio in Montreal. Note the pile of books holding up the heavy iron curling "stone."**

*Notman Photographic Archives, McCord Museum of Canadian History , Montreal, #II-23555.*

**Mrs. Russell Stephenson poses for a curling composite photo at the Notman Studio in Montreal. She gains assistance from the broom in holding her pose.**

*Notman Photographic Archives, McCord Museum of Canadian History , Montreal, #II-23560.*

**The composite photo of Miss Allen and Mrs. Stephenson curling in 1876. Note that the books holding up the stone have been removed, and a painted outdoor scene has been added, as has a sheet of zinc to simulate the ice, and lamb's wool, slightly out of focus, to simulate snow.**

*Notman Photographic Archives, McCord Museum of Canadian History , Montreal, #II-23640.*

Notman was also a master of combining any number of single images into a photographic composite. Take the three photos of Miss Allen (alone), Mrs. Stephenson (alone), and the two of them combined, in an early "action" shot.

Perhaps Notman's most famous curling photo was the one he composed in 1877. As well as being a fine photographer, Notman was also an outstanding businessman—witness this announcement from November of that year.

"Having been invited by the commissioners to send an exhibit to the Paris Exhibition," wrote Notman (on the sketch of the photo), "we have decided to set up a large picture 'Curling in Canada' and for that purpose have prepared a large sketch of what is intended. We want to solicit your cooperation in this undertaking and will be glad if you will call and see the cartoon."

The fact that Governor General Lord Dufferin (an avid curler) and Lady Dufferin, together with Prime Minister Sir John A. Macdonald (and Mrs.

**Hold it!**

*John Dunnett cartoon, courtesy* Canadian Curling News

"Hold it!"

Macdonald), would be in the photo, along with such other pillars of Montreal society as Sir Hugh Allan, Sir A. T. Galt, and Sir E. Selby Smith, helped attract those who wished to be a part of the finished endeavour. Or at least a part of that strata of society.

Technology has continued to provide better photographic techniques. But it is still the photographer's eye, his or her intuition and anticipation of a moment in time, that helps provide the most dramatic shots—shots that remove the need for a thousand words of explanation.

In addition to the photographs in this book, there are a number of drawings, cartoons and illustrations all designed to help us appreciate the history of the game in Canada.

*Doug Maxwell, 2002*

CHAPTER 1

# Golden Daze

**Thursday, February 21, 2002, dawned bright in Utah, and with a warmth unusual** for February. After ten days of Olympic curling, the Canadian women's team of skip Kelley Law, third Julie Skinner, second Georgina Wheatcroft, and lead Diane Nelson arrived at the arena—the Ice Sheet in Ogden—early, much earlier than they had originally planned, or dreamed.

The previous day, after finishing the preliminary round-robin in first place (eight wins, one loss) they had played the fourth-place finisher from Great Britain, skipped by Rhona Martin. To their dismay and consternation, they lost the semifinal and, this day, instead of playing a gold medal game in the afternoon, they were in a morning game for the bronze. Playing Kari Erickson's foursome from the USA, they were able to shut out their Wednesday disappointment and refocus their energies. They won the game, 9-5, and the bronze medal that went with the win. Truth to tell, it was welcome—what medal isn't—but still, it was scant consolation for the wished-for gold that had been confidently predicted for them prior to the XIX Winter Games.

That afternoon, the conquering skip of the previous day, Rhona Martin of Scotland, drew her final stone of the final end of the final game to the button, and gave Great Britain its first gold medal in nineteen years of Winter Olympic

**The gold they had planned for turned into bronze for Canada's 2002 Olympic women's team. Showing off their medals are (l-r) alternate Cheryl Noble, lead Diane Nelson, second Georgina Wheatcroft, third Julie Sutton, and skip Kelley Law.**

*Photo by Boyd Ivey.*

participation. It was also the first-ever curling medal of any colour for British women. In Britain, jubilation and exhilaration exploded for Martin's team of Janice Rankin, Fiona MacDonald, Debbie Knox, and alternate Margaret Morton. It was more than a golden moment; it was a vindication of Scotland's place in the world of curling, and of Scotland's role as the birthplace of curling.

Friday, February 22, 2002, in Utah was crisp and pleasant. Kevin Martin and his team of Don Walchuk, Carter Rycroft, and Don Bartlett were confident that their quest to win the first-ever official Canadian men's curling gold medal would be successful. After all, they had finished atop the ten-team round-robin series with eight wins and only one loss.

An athlete's Olympic dream: posing for photos when the medals are handed out. At the Salt Lake City Winter Games of 2002, the Canadian men, middle row, celebrate their silver medal. From l-r are Kevin Martin (skip), Carter Rycroft (second), Don Walchuk (third), Don Bartlett (lead), and Ken Tralnberg (alternate). The gold medal team from Norway, skipped by Pål Trulsen (left rear), join in the celebration, together with the Swiss bronze medallists, led by Andreas Schwaller, in front.

*Photo by Boyd Ivey.*

They had been the favourites from the start, and as the best team from a country with over a million curlers (more than 1,300 clubs) the numbers appeared to be on their side. While Martin's quartet was winning its semifinal against an old nemesis, Peter (Peja) Lindholm of Sweden, Norway's Pål Trulsen was qualifying for the final by downing Switzerland's Andreas Schwaller. The comparisons between Martin and Trulsen, between Canada and Norway, couldn't have been more stark.

Trulsen was representing a country whose major winter sports were skiing, ski jumping, and speed skating. Curling, with less than a thousand players all told (fewer than twenty clubs) barely registered on Norway's consciousness.

And while Trulsen was an experienced international player, most thought that the final game, while it would be tough, would belong to Canada.

The game was tense and tight. It would be decided, as was the case in the women's final, by the last stone of the last end. Except this time, it would be different. Martin's final granite, with the gold on the line, ground to a halt an inch too far, and the Norwegian underdogs, with the steal of a single point, claimed the gold, 6-5. Canada had to be content with silver. Many less-than-knowledgeable Canadians wondered how a country with so many curlers could be defeated by a country with so few. Perhaps the answer lies in the subtleties and peculiar appeal of a game that is at once highly competitive, highly sociable, and highly open to upsets.

The Olympics is not about which country has the most curlers, or even the best curlers. It is about which country has the best team on the day of the final, which one is best able to focus on the task at hand, which one is best able to calm its own jitters and force the adrenalin of a gold-medal game into the perfection of play.

As Canadians were commiserating over Martin's loss, some Norwegians were offering silent thanks to Canadians past and present who had been of help to the small curling nation. Almost twenty-five years before Salt Lake, in 1978 to be exact, a Norwegian team skipped by Kristian Sørum had eliminated the favoured Canadians (led by Ed Lukowich and Mike Chernoff) in a semifinal of the Air Canada Silver Broom World Championship in Winnipeg. The head official that day was Ray Turnbull, who, on a number of occasions, had taken his curling expertise to Europe and held clinics that helped the Norwegians (and others) to become more proficient at the game. As Turnbull stood at one corner of the rink that day, watching Norway beat Canada 6-2, one leather-lunged fan in the upper reaches of the arena yelled down at him, "It's all your fault Turnbull!"

"I took it as a compliment," Turnbull later declared.

In 2002, a fan might have been forgiven if, following the Norwegian victory in Ogden, he or she had yelled "It's all your fault Lino," in reference to Lino Di Iorio of Richmond Hill, Ontario. Di Iorio became a curler (and a fan of all things

**Lino Di Iorio, curling innovator extraordinaire.**
*Photo courtesy* Canadian Curling News.

curling) later than most, but he made up for lost time by turning his inventive mind and manufacturing smarts into a series of curling developments. There was his "hole in the sole" Teflon slider, his computer software designed to assist in developing a better delivery, and his modified radar gun that helped teams develop a more consistent release of the stone. Among his followers were the Norwegians, led by Pål Trulsen and team, and the president of the Norwegian Curling Association, Kristian Sørum. While Sørum did not win the World final in 1978, he did the following year, in Berne, Switzerland. It was Norway's first world championship. Now the Norwegians were on the verge of Olympic victory.

It wasn't the first time, nor would it be the last, that Canadian curlers had helped smaller curling countries. Not only has Canada sent curling emissaries abroad, it has also opened up its elite training centres to other countries' teams and has become a mecca for many curlers. In doing so, it has emulated the Scots who, in the late eighteenth century and early nineteenth century, exported their game to Canada.

If Scotland is the birthplace of curling, then surely Canada is its cradle, and the country to which all curlers now look for inspiration in building the sport.

The Canadian players in Utah were part of a much larger team. There were alternates Cheryl Noble and Ken Tralnberg; team coaches Gene Friesen (Law) and Jules Owchar (Martin); national coaches Jim Waite (men) and Lindsay Sparkes (women); and Canadian Curling Association Team Leader, Gerry Peckham. And, along with family and friends of the teams, cheering from the sidelines, was Canadian Olympic Association Director (and past president of the CCA) Pat Reid.

Canada's teams, like those of other countries, had physiotherapists and psychologists among their supporters, all there to provide specific and enthusiastic support for Canada's teams as they took to the ice in their quest for gold.

On the ice, the Canadians were on their own. It would be their decisions, their shots, their ability to withstand the Olympic pressure that would decide the outcome. There were no time outs allowed, so there could be no coaching conferences. But the Canadian teams were experienced, internationally savvy foursomes. Both the Martin and Law teams had survived a gruelling ten-team Olympic Trial series two months earlier in Regina: both were primed to win.

The 2,000-seat Ice Sheet had been sold out for almost a year. Almost half the seats had been set aside for members of "the Olympic Family" and, more often than not, many of those seats would be empty. But the seats for wives, husbands, friends and supporters were filled, and they provided an enthusiastic cheering section for all teams. Among the spectators at the men's gold-medal game (Norway vs Canada) was King Harald V of Norway, a presence at once distinguished and austere.

The World Curling Federation, in charge of the myriad technical details for the curling (ice-makers, officials, public relations staff) occupied a number of seats, both backstage and out front. Media from all over the world were shoe-horned into one end at a media bench. There were photographers, technical advisors, electricians, carpenters, and arena staff in attendance.

And security.

The Atlanta Summer Olympics (four times the size of the Winter Games) spent over $100 million on security. In Salt Lake, in the wake of the September 11 terrorist attack five months earlier, security cost upwards of $300 million.

CBC-TV had a large crew on hand, as did NBC-TV, who hired Canadian commentators Don Chevrier and Don Duguid to explain the game. Don Wittman, CBC's veteran Olympic sportscaster, was flanked in the television booth by former Olympians Joan McCusker, a member of Sandra Schmirler's gold-medal team from 1998, and Mike Harris, skip of the 1998 men's silver-medal team. The television coverage from Ogden was seen by millions around the world. When it came time for the women's and men's finals, the BBC and

Norwegian Television pre-empted their regular late-night programming to show each final live to huge audiences. Teams that had been unknown only days before became household names overnight, and when Great Britain's Rhona Martin won the gold medal with a 4-3, last-stone victory over Switzerland, Scotland and all of Great Britain rejoiced. The television audience at midnight in Great Britain numbered over six million viewers, a BBC record.

Similarly, there was an electrifying response in Norway when Trulsen edged Canada for the gold, 6-5. Suddenly, curling became front-page news. Norwegians rejoiced in a gold earned in a sport other than skiing and clamoured to learn more about the game.

In the United States, an unprecedented numbers of viewers, new to the game, flocked to their local club to learn more. Two people from Florida, one month after the Games, drove across country to attend the World Championships in Bismarck, North Dakota, so intrigued were they with curling!

The year 2002 marked the fourth time curling had been present in the post-World War II Olympics. In 1988 and 1992, curling was a demonstration sport. In 1998, curling became a medal sport, and in 2002, Canada had a chance to make curling history. Never before had one country been able to so dominate the sport as to win two Olympic gold medals. Canadians were confident that 2002 was their year to do so. After the Canadian women had been denied gold, the pressure on the men increased exponentially. Still, they were confident that their golden moment was at hand.

It was not to be. Canada would have to be content with silver and bronze.

But if the gold medals were, for Canada, agonizingly absent, the sport itself was impressively present. How curling in Canada has reached this point is the subject of this book. Nowhere else in the world is the game of curling so pervasive, so important, or so enjoyable to so many, as it is in Canada.

CHAPTER 2

# Early Days

**In the middle of the seventeenth century, the British Isles were hit with a climate** change that came to be known as The Little Ice Age. In 1684, the Thames River froze to a thickness of 11 inches [28 cm]. In 1709, the seas around Scotland were frozen for miles offshore. In winter, the ground was so hard that it was impossible to put a shovel into the earth. The small, smoky, and drafty cottages in Scotland offered little protection from the cold. So Scots farmers looked for activities that could help them endure the frigid winter months.

Ball games were impossible, but, thanks to the frozen streams and lochs and the abundance of channel stones, curling was born. The usually accepted date for the earliest game—a far cry from the curling of today—is 1541, when a curling challenge was issued, in Latin, by one John Slater to Gavin Hamilton. However, the famous Stirling stone, discovered near the town of Stirling, with the date 1511 chiselled into it, suggests an even earlier start of the game.

Two hundred or so years later, curling came to Canada, with the 78th Fraser Highlanders, who were a part of Wolfe's army in the drive to capture Quebec. The standard story is that the Frasers, shortly after the battle of Ste. Foy in 1759, and wanting a diversion, sought permission to melt down cannonballs and turn them into metal curling stones—or irons, as they would become known.

**One theory of the origin of iron curling stones suggests that in 1759 the 78th Fraser Highlanders removed the metal hub caps from cannons (similar to this one being aimed by Arnold Richardson 200 years later), inserted handles, and began curling at Quebec City.**

*Photo by Michael Burns.*

It's a colourful and delightful story, and has taken on a stature of almost mythical proportions. It is also, not to put too fine a point on it, probably inaccurate. In spite of diligent primary research by a number of curlers and historians, there is no proof of the cannonball story. Think about it for a minute, and you may see four major reasons it appears unlikely. First, it seems a little far-fetched that a commanding officer would give permission to dispose of even a part of his ammunition supply so soon after a victory. Secondly, consider how difficult it would be to build a fire of such heat that it could melt heavy cannonballs (the first forge in Canada, in Sherbrooke, was not built until a few years later). Thirdly, if the cannonballs could not be melted, could they have been cut in two, assuming the soldiers could gain permission to do so? That, too, appears unlikely, since to do so would require considerable power and some form of machinery. And finally, is there a better explanation? For of a certainty, irons did exist. So if not from cannonballs, then from whence came iron curling stones?

In their book, *Sports and Games in Canadian Life, 1700 to the Present*, Maxwell L. Howell and Nancy Howell offer a slightly more prosaic, but also more likely, answer. They suggest that the circular, metal-rimmed hubcaps of gun carriages, with handles inserted, became the first irons that introduced curling to North America. It seems a better explanation than any other. Whatever the facts, and however they were fashioned, it is indisputable that iron curling "stones," shaped like tea kettles and weighing about 60 to 80 pounds [27 to 36 kg] each, for men—40 to 48 pounds [18 to 21 kg] for women—were the first stones to be used in the latter half of the eighteenth century. Only in Canada, you say? Yes, 'twas only in Canada that irons appeared. There are no records, in Scotland or anywhere else, indi-

cating iron stones. When twenty merchants in Montreal elected to form the Montreal Curling Club in 1807, they used irons exclusively. (That's not all that was exclusive, incidentally; the members were handpicked—no others need apply.) The Montreal Curling Club and 1807 are both significant: that curling club became the first organized sporting club in North America. Irons were used in Montreal and throughout the Ottawa Valley until the mid-1900s. Today they can be found in various parts of the country in trophy cases, as hog-line sentinels, as historical curios, or even doorstops at the local club.

The melted cannonball theory, as colourful as it is, may have a modicum of fact associated with it, but not relevant to 1759. Try sixty years later in 1819, some twelve years after the founding of the Montreal Curling Club. In the *History of Argenteuil County*, *The Canal Records*, it is recorded that the Royal

**The thrill of irons curling is kept alive with an annual match in Montreal featuring contemporary members of the 78th Fraser Highlanders.**

*Photo courtesy Macdonald Stewart Foundation.*

Staff Corps, comprised mostly of Scots soldiers, was commissioned to build a canal around the Long-Sault rapids. Being Scots, they curled on the river in the winter, and were much envied by the Scots of Lachute, who issued a challenge to the military. The problem was that there were not enough stones available for a game, so the decision was made to order a set of granites from Scotland.

If the Scottish stones had arrived in time, the course of curling history might have been different. But the ship carrying the stones ran aground off Newfoundland and sank. All was lost, and since there was not enough time to order a new set before winter, it appeared that the challenge match would have to wait another year. But that was not an option to the soldiers. They would have to find a substitute for the granites that resided somewhere off the Grand Banks.

Someone in the regiment came up with the idea of melting old cannonballs to create the same kind of irons in use at the Montreal Club, official approval was given, and the games were rescheduled. And this time the cannonball concept worked. A blacksmith working for the Carillon and Grenville Canal company, James Wood, saw the commercial potential in these irons. Rather than depend on a supply of old cannonballs, he prepared a mold that would allow the casting of an iron "stone" that would weigh between 58 and 62 pounds [26 and 28 kg]. Later, the Victoria Foundry of Lachute took over the task and, in one season alone, Wood sold over a thousand irons at a cost of three dollars each.

Even today, when irons are only a memory, exhibition games are played at Montreal's Stewart Museum on Ile Sainte-Hélène by members of the Olde 78th Fraser Highlanders.

The Howells also provided a Canadian answer to "Why curling?" that echoes W. H. Murray of Scotland, whose book *The Curling Companion* is of great interest to the curling historian. The Howells write that "the years before Confederation were years of hardship, travail, hunger, disappointments, disasters, wars and terror on the one hand, and ingenuity, settlement and comradeship on the other. Against this patchwork background, we can picture the life of the times. Work, more work, and still more work gave birth to the desire to find means of relieving the drudgery and monotony of life. As a result, the central core of life seems to have been an atmosphere of gay sociability combined with a quest for new and daring experiences" (54).

There were many reasons that brought British immigrants to Canada. For those who were suffering at home, Canada offered a new start. So the Scottish Clearances, the Potato Famine in Ireland, the upheaval caused by the industrial revolution in England all conspired to provide a second chance for many. For those who still had some wealth, but saw it diminishing, Canada offered a chance to build on that wealth. It was said that in the Canada of Victorian times it was difficult not to make money if you were willing to work hard. And so they came, bringing their customs and sports—including curling—with them.

In addition to those Scottish newcomers who had some curling in their background, there were others who wanted to help alleviate the long winters with some kind of sporting activity, and wondered if curling might be the way

## CURLING TOO MUCH OF A NATIONAL INSTITUTION

"Of all the 'national games', properly so called, none have more devoted partisans than curling. The Scotsman prides himself upon that game as being peculiarly his own. To the indifferent on-looker, especially if he is not a Caledonian, and has heard nothing of the mysteries and the technicalities of curling, the spectacle is indeed an odd one, to see something approaching to a dozen, apparently rational, men frisking about on the ice, some of them with brooms in their hands, others tossing mighty stones along a previously prepared track, and all watching anxiously to see where the 'halt' will be made. But curling is too much of a national institution in Canada to require any special description. In fact, we believe the game is better known in this country than in many parts of Scotland. It is a healthful, refreshing exercise and when topped off with a dinner of 'beef and greens' offers one of the most pleasant modes, out of all the variety which our bracing Canadian climate affords, of spending a winter's afternoon. On the 17th of last month the Thistle Club, of this city [Montreal], opened a new rink on the upper end of St. Monique Street, and our artist has given an illustration of the proceedings."

*Source: excerpt from the* Canadian Illustrated News, *January 14, 1871*

to do so. In 1883, a Fredericton, NB, shopkeeper, John Neill, was shown a copy of the *Glasgow Herald* by one of his customers, who pointed out a six-column story on curling in Scotland. The customer, Ludlow Robinson, asked if it would not be possible to obtain curling stones from Scotland and start the game locally. Although they could enlist only about seven members at the start, Neill and Ludlow persisted, trying to play on Heron's Lake and the Naskwaak River. They finally asked the colonel of the local regiment if they could make ice on the parade ground, and permission was granted—provided they used the gravel road and not the grass. It was arduous work. They tried drilling a well to get water for the ice, but that didn't work. Instead, they hauled casks of water on sleds. Eventually the club flourished.

No matter where they settled in their new country, the newcomers found weather similar to what they had left behind, but on a larger scale. It was hotter in the summer and colder in the winter. If, in the larger towns and cities, there was ample opportunity for cricket in the summer months, then the winter months, they soon discovered, were longer—and harder—than in Britain. For those of Scottish heritage, the long Canadian winters meant more time for curling on the lakes, ponds, and streams that speckled the landscape.

In addition to the merchants who took up curling in town and village, there were also the Scottish gold miners who introduced the game into the interior of British Columbia, and in an echo that sounded half a world away, in the South Island of New Zealand. The difference in climate, however, doomed curling's growth in New Zealand to be slow and patchy, while the Canadian growth surged.

Over the many years there were high points in the growth of curling in Canada, and plateaus that marked spurts of the sport. Changes included the move from outdoor ice to covered rinks; the growth of friendly matches between adjacent towns; the advent of artificial ice; the building of roads and railway and the growth of communication; eventually regional and provincial competition and then national championships; world championships; and the Olympics.

Curling had become an essential element of grassroots Canada. Through its long history, it became a sport attractive to all levels of society, all ages of participants—a lifetime persuasion.

# CHAPTER 3

# The Fergus Curling Club, a Canadian Story in Miniature

**Since the early 1800s, two Ontario clubs, the Fergus Curling Club and the** Kingston Curling Club, have maintained a friendly argument about which is the longest-running in Ontario. Kingston's claim as the first club in the province is undeniable, having been founded in 1820. The Fergus club wasn't founded until 1834. This was four years before the founding of the Grand Caledonian Curling Club in Scotland, seven years later to become the Royal Caledonian Curling Club, the Mother Club of curling. At some time between then and now, the Kingston club suspended operations, so while Kingston can rightly claim to be the oldest club in Ontario, Fergus can quietly (and with just the hint of a wink) state that it is the oldest *continuously operating* club in the province.

While this chapter tells the story of the Fergus club in southern Ontario, a simple change of name to that of any other community with a club, anywhere else in Canada, would duplicate, in many particulars, the experience of clubs that were springing up wherever there was winter ice. Let us, then, use the story of the Fergus club as a template for the founding and development of many other clubs across the land. Emery Nelson's fine book *One Hundred and Fifty Years of Curling: The Fergus Curling Club*, helps to tell the story.

In March of 1834, Hugh Black Sr. and his extended family of thirteen departed Scotland. They arrived in Fergus in late summer. Black was a highly respected farmer from Perthshire and, on arrival as one of the first settlers in Fergus (named after its founder, Adam Fergusson), was persuaded to open a tavern, which soon became the focal point of the small community. An able entrepreneur, he also introduced an ox-drawn stagecoach which carried passengers, and produce, to Hamilton and back in four days. The journey today takes about an hour and a half.

Having curled in Scotland, it was natural that Black, with four of his sons and two sons-in-law, would organize a curling club in the fall of 1834. Since they could not import stones from Scotland, they discovered, while building a barn, that wooden blocks would slide nicely across the ice, so one of them turned bird's-eye maple blocks into curling stones for use along the frozen street outside Black's Tavern. In a manner similar to today's promotional efforts by breweries, the move ensured a longer stay at the tavern, and presumably, greater sales.

After a couple of winters curling "between the stumps on the main street," and as the town continued to grow, the games were shifted to the Washing Green, where sheep were washed before shearing, on the south side of the Grand River. At this time, games were won by the first team to reach 31 points, and games were conducted with eight players a side, each throwing one stone an end. Members had to be invited to join the club and had to pass a form of initiation before being accepted.

In 1842, a dam was constructed to provide curling ice, but it lasted only until 1845, when another dam was constructed—at a cost of six dollars. The canny Scots paid half the cost when the dam was built and the balance when it was certain the dam would hold! In 1846, several members donated materials for an 18' x 12' [5.4 x 3.6 m] curling hut to house the stones, and a "building bee" saw the curling house raised in a day.

In the beginning, all games were local and were played in the heart of the community, since there were no railroads, and roads were little more than rough trails through the bush. As the roads improved, they were able to venture outside the community, but only after considerable planning. Brooms and stones had to be transported. Shovels, for clearing the snow, were essential. Travel was by sleigh or wagon, pulled by a horse or oxen, and there was much walking through mud, water, and snow. Keeping warm was always a problem.

Much thought was given to the nature of the various matches. There was an annual Married Men vs Bachelors match as well as a game between the Grits and Tories. The losers had to provide a meal of oysters for the winners. In 1847, an ecclesiastical split led to the formation of the Auld Kirk and the Free Kirk, and when religious animosities had cooled down sufficiently, the two groups engaged in an annual New Year's Day match. Games were usually followed by the traditional

In 1897, these double rink members from Carleton Place were the Central Canada Curling Association champions. One of the few photos to list the members of the team with their occupations, it is possible to discern here the elite of Carleton Place. Front row (l-r): Robert Patterson, barrister; Rev. Robert McNair, Minister, St. Andrews Church. Back row (l-r): David Moffatt, planing mill and building contractor; A. H. Edwards, lumber manufacturer; A. R. G. Peden, town clerk; Hugh M. Williams, lumber manufacturer; John Adams Bangs, manager, Bank of Ottawa; John C. Switzer, druggist.

*Pelton C.C., National Archives of Canada, C-001340.*

"Beef and Greens" dinner and, often, the payment, by the losers, of a barrel of oatmeal for the poor. Inevitably there was a long program of postdinner speeches, toasts, and songs.

By 1883, the matches included a challenge by The Professionals (doctors and lawyers) against the Bankers, and when the Professionals won, they agreed to a further challenge from the Hotel Keepers. The Professionals won again.

Within twenty years from the formation of that first club in Fergus, fourteen more clubs had been established in the area, and with the coming of the railroad, inter-club matches were begun. Throughout this period strict adherence to the rules of behaviour was required. The story is told of one skip who, in

1851, complained after one of his matches about the poor play of his team. His intemperate remarks prompted a club meeting at which he was fined two shillings, sixpence, for "using unbecoming language to the members of the club, for having no respect for the club, and for refusing to attend the disciplinary meeting" (Nelson 9). It is presumed he paid the fine and remained a club member, for some time later, he was named an honorary member.

By 1870, the Fergus curlers were eager to build a covered facility, but it wasn't until 1879 that a two-sheet rink came into being. In 1883, a season's ticket for curlers (which included skating on adjacent ice) cost three dollars.

In 1909, the Diamond Jubilee of the club was celebrated with a bonspiel that attracted teams from all across southern and western Ontario. First prize was a diamond ring for each member of the winning side. The sociability of the occasion was properly observed, and one rink, from Grand Rapids, Michigan, even brought a curling stone banquet table centrepiece, constructed of carnations, with a green foliage handle.

A new arena for hockey and curling was opened in 1928, although a blizzard made it impossible for many local or out-of-town visitors to attend the ceremonies. Still, over six hundred people braved the blizzard and were present for the festivities.

The club's Centennial Bonspiel, slated for January 9, 1934, attracted teams from more than twenty-five communities (entry fee six dollars). However, "the January thaw" spoiled the plans—and the ice—and the games had to be postponed until January 15. To prove that the vagaries of curling seldom change, the game was in doubt to the final stones. Emery Nelson recounts the story (21).

"A Fergus rink," he writes, "skipped by E. C. Codling with O. B. Brown, J. J. Rutherford and A. C. Deacon won the Centennial Competition. In the last end the B. E. Bitz rink from Durham was up by three shots. E. C. Codling threw a hard running shot, cleaning out all the Durham stones and staying in the house, thereby leaving Fergus lying five. First prize consisted of four gold medals and four electric floor polishers."

**This diagram of a memorable shot, from the Fergus Centennial Bonspiel of 1934, proves that not all the sensational shots occur only in current curling. With his last stone, and trailing Durham by three points, skip E.C. Codling of Fergus threw a hard running shot, removed all three Durham stones, and counted five for the championship!**

*Diagram courtesy Emery Nelson.*

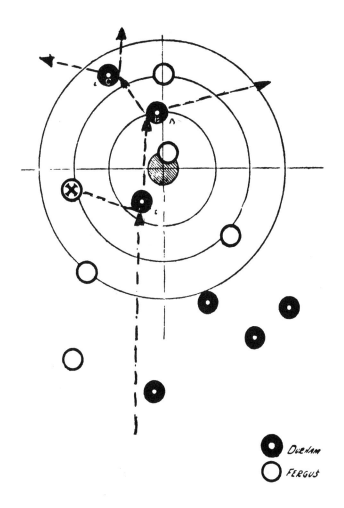

Durham
Fergus

In 1950, the club agreed to change from an all-male membership to include women, provided the women formed a club and requested permission to curl. The women waited four years to make their request known, and in 1954 were warmly welcomed, at a fee of five dollars per member. They were allowed use of the club two afternoons a week, plus Friday nights.

From the beginning, individual members were responsible for providing their own stones. It wasn't till the mid-1930s that the idea of a club purchasing a full set of matched stones became popular. In Toronto, the occasion of the arrival of the first set of matched rocks in Ontario, at the Toronto Curling Club, was marked by a celebration that included a panoramic photo of club members, together with the new stones, freshly arrived from Scotland.

Before leaving the Fergus Curling Club, perhaps we should consider the speech of William Weems, as set out in John A. Stevenson's book *Curling in Ontario, 1846–1946* (57–59). Of all the many thousands of words that have been written about curling, perhaps none capture the essence of the sport as do those of Weems.

It seems that Weems, before emigrating to Canada, had been a shepherd in the Grampian Mountains in Scotland. He settled in Fergus and was an ardent curler, and would skip one of the teams in the annual New Year's Day match between the Auld Kirk and the Free Kirk.

But let Stevenson take up the story: "As skip of the Auld Kirk," he writes, "[Weems] managed to win the match by one shot with his last stone of the last end. At the banquet that followed he made, in reply to a toast proposed by the Hon. Adam Ferguson, a remarkable speech, . . . as recorded by Mr. Logan Perry in his book *This Toon o' Mine*." (For those whose knowledge of Scots dialect is wanting, there is a "translation" on succeeding pages.)

"Sir Adam Drummond and friends," recounts Perry, of Weems' words, "I ha'e tae thank you. I am getting' gey auld and stiff and ye ken I'm no guid at speakin'. The tapple tursie o' work has been mine maist of ma days with a day's play noo and then—wi' the bools in simmer and the curlin' in winter. And of a' the mony games I ha'e played since comin' tae this country, this day's game caps them a' for rale curling. The ice was fine and the drawin' grand. And of a' the shots for steady winnin' gi'e me a canny draw. I'll no misca a frisky run whiles, if we could a' dae it like Whistlewood or Mattha there. And let me tell you there were no mony chips or wicks missed by either of them this day. The game was oors at the end, to be sure, but with naething to brag o'. Anither breath and the Free Kirk would be sitting here and us there the nicht.

"There's no game like curling. It's an honest sensible game. It's an honest couthie game is curling, that we Kirk folk are a better for taking a spiel at whiles. And forbye there's muckle o' life to learn frae it. We a' ken the slips and fa's in it, the chancy shots and a' that. When ower muckle room is gi'en a stane and it gangs birlin' awa' through the hoose, a waif strae whiles will grip the bottom o't and drag it to a stop on the snuff. We've a' seen that. Anither stane cast asklant will whiles lose its turn and wind in shankshaped tae the very bit. But anither stane cast exactly tae the broom will no come near the bit. And whiles the maist

When the first set of matched stones in Ontario arrived at the Toronto Curling Club in 1938, it was a time for celebration, and the whole club turned out to record the occasion.

*Photo courtesy* Canadian Curling News.

OFFICIAL OPENING OF THE TOR
THE CLUB'S NEW "KAY EXCELSI

carefu' o' curlers will slip their foot oot o' the hackie and spil a'. These things ha'e happened this day and it's my belief that sic mishaps are aye gaun on ilka day in the game of life. As Robbie Burns says, 'the best laid plans o' mice and men gang aft agley.' Aye dae they. Aye, my friends, like the game o' life, the game o' curling is a chancy struggle at best. In the middle of the game o' life we meet wi' disappointments, we fecht for bread, we wrangle, we play pranks and we chase baubles. Near the end o't, in the glimmer o' auld age, we dream dreams o' the

CURLING CLUB, NOV. 18th 1938.
ATCHED CURLING STONES IN FOREGROUND.

game we hae played. At last we slip awa' like the snaw in a thaw: to foregather aroon the Great Tee abune, and oor ain bit place here is kent nae mair forever."

There's a postscript: It seems that after all the speeches had been finished, all the songs sung and the evening's sociability was over, Weems set out to walk to his modest cottage where he lived alone. "He had almost reached it when the runner of a cutter drawn by a fractious horse struck him and hurled him into a snowbank," writes Stevenson. "Struggling to his feet, he was just able to reach his home, where, being badly hurt, he slumped into his old armchair near the fireplace. Next morning a neighbour found him still seated in it, but dead, and holding in his hand a miniature portrait of his beloved wife, who had passed away many years before."

The story embodies so many of the elements of early curling that is easy to miss them unless reminded. It is a story of Scots who had come to Canada to make a new life, and who knew well the history and traditions of the game that reminded them of their former home. It was a game that entailed a concern for the less fortunate, and a sociable game in which respect for opponents was a given. The sociability of the occasion was usually enlivened by a banquet after the match, where toasts were proposed and answered with much feeling and eloquence.

As William Weems put it a hundred and fifty and more years ago, "there's nae game like curling. It's an honest sensible game . . . an honest couthie game is curling."

Today's curlers are surely nodding their heads in agreement.

Now, here is the Weems speech, translated from Scots to Canadian.

"Sir Adam Drummond and friends, I have to thank you. I am getting very old and stiff and you know I'm no good at speakin'. The topsie turvy of work has been mine most of my days with a day's play now and then—with lawn bowling in summer and curling in winter. And of all the many games I have played since coming to this country, this day's game caps them all for real curling. The ice was fine and the drawing grand. And of all the shots for steady winning give me a canny draw. I'd try a frisky running shot sometimes if I could do it like Whistlewood or Mattha. And let me tell you, there were not many chips or wicks missed by either of them this day. The game was ours at the end, to be sure, but with nothing to brag about. Another breath and the Free Kirk would be sitting here and us there tonight.

"There's no game like curling. It's an honest sensible game. It's an honest, agreeable game is curling, that we Church folk are all the better for playing in a bonspiel sometimes. And yes, there's much of life to learn from it. We all know the slips and falls in it, the chancy shots and all that. When too much broom is given and the stone looks to go whirling through the house, a stray straw will sometimes grip the bottom of the stone and drag it to a stop on the button. We've all seen that. Another stone thrown badly will lose its turn and wind up in great shape, while another stone delivered exactly to the broom will not come near the target. And sometimes the most careful of curlers will slip in the hack and fall down. These things have happened this day and it's my belief that such mishaps are always a part of the game of life. As Robbie Burns says, 'the best laid plans o' mice and men gang aft agley.' Yes they do. Yes, my friends, like the game of life, the game of curling is a chancy struggle at best. In the middle of the game of life we meet with disappointments, we work hard for bread, we wrangle, we play pranks and we chase baubles. Near the end of it, in the glimmer of old age, we dream dreams of the games we have played. At last we slip away like the snow in a thaw: to foregather around the Great Tee above, and our own small place here is known no more."

# CHAPTER 4

# Westward Ho

**Perhaps Horace Greeley, the famous US editor, was a closet curler. How else** to explain his famous dictum "Go west, young man, go west"? For it was in western Canada that curling experienced its greatest expansion. If curling in the East was an elitist, merchant-driven sport (and it was), and if curling in the West started in a similar way (and it did), it soon would become a democratic sport in the West, a game for everyone.

When the last spike of the Canadian Pacific Railway was driven in 1885, the CPR set out to convert much of the land it had been given into farm land. Its immigration efforts, particularly in Great Britain, Europe, and the Ukraine helped open up the West. And as settlers moved from eastern Canada and the United States to join those from overseas, curling tagged along and quickly became a staple of the new villages and towns.

Winnipeg became the hub of the game. Indeed, to many Canadians (and all Winnipeggers), it is still regarded as the epicentre of curling, worldwide. In 1876, the year after Sir John A. Macdonald became Canada's first Prime Minister, Manitoba's first curling club was formed, in Winnipeg. December 11th saw the first match held there and, as was the custom, the losers were required to donate a barrel of oatmeal to the hospital. In 1879, a game between the City Fathers and

the "Ordinary People" was won by the latter, and the aldermen on the losing side were required to pay a forfeit of an oyster dinner. (Why an oyster dinner? No one seems to know. The assumption is that oysters, in Manitoba, were difficult to obtain, expensive, and therefore highly prized. What better way to gently rub salt in a wound than to savour a victory while slurping down oysters at a post-game banquet?)

That same year, 1879, saw the first curling in Saskatchewan, in Prince Albert, Rosthern, and Battleford. It would be another ten years before curling arrived in Regina.

**Howard (Pappy) Wood, like most curlers, never lost his zest for the game. This photo was taken as he was about to embark on his 53rd consecutive appearance in the famed Manitoba Bonspiel.**

*Photo by Hugh Allan, courtesy Western Canada Pictorial Index.*

The first bonspiel in Winnipeg, in 1884, was the forerunner of the famed Manitoba Bonspiel, perhaps the best-known curling competition in the world, which was begun in 1889, the year after the formation of the Manitoba Branch of the Royal Caledonia Curling Club (RCCC). Sixty-two teams spent three days at that first event. All but the most necessary of activities stopped during "The Bonspiel." Commercial activity was focused on "The Bonspiel." For the farming community, it was a chance to come to the city and match wits on the ice with the "slickers." It was reported that, at one time, even the sitting of the Manitoba Legislature had to be cancelled because too many of the Members were attending "The Bonspiel" and it was not possible to obtain a quorum! Today, The January Bonspiel attracts teams from all over the curling world for more than a week of high-level competition, fun, and sociability. In 1988, to help celebrate the centennial of the famed event, a total of 1,280 teams began play in all the clubs in and around the city.

In Alberta, the first curling club was formed in Lethbridge in 1887. Although there had been curling in Calgary since 1885, it wasn't until 1888 that the Calgary Curling Club was formally brought into being, and became affiliated with the Manitoba Branch of the RCCC. Edmonton began its curling in the same year—1888. In 1889, curling came to Macleod, Banff, and Anthracite. The arrival of the railroad not only helped open up the foothills, but it also made travel between curling centres that much easier. Curling was booming.

**Curling has long been a mainstay among members of the Canadian Armed Forces. This photo shows a match at 5th Infantry Brigade headquarters in January of 1919. During WW II, it was rumoured that several curling stones were sent from Scotland, via the Red Cross, to POW camps in Germany.**
*National Archives of Canada, PA-003914.*

It was Scots miners who brought the game to the interior of British Columbia toward the end of the nineteenth century. The first club was formed in Kaslo in 1895, and within three years, the Kootenay Curling Association played host to a bonspiel that drew eighteen teams from Rossland, Sandon, Revelstoke, and Kaslo.

In 1830, the total number of acres granted to a variety of newcomers was as follows:

- to militia, discharged soldiers, and pensioners—18,900 acres
- to officers—12,600 acres
- to United Empire Loyalists—27,400 acres
- to others—9,336 acres

The average price per acre at that time was four shillings, nine pence.

*Source: Catharine Parr Traill,* The Backwoods of Canada, *(360).*

In 1896, when gold was discovered at Bonanza Creek in the Yukon Territory, thousands went rushing to the Chilkoot Pass on their way (so they thought) to fame and fortune. And while it is known that some of the heaviest items carried up the mountain pass, piece by piece, included a piano, there is no known report of curling stones being so carried. But they were there, as can be seen in early photos.

Curling in Canada has always been aligned, historically, with the military, and their early offshoot, the police force. It was the military that brought curling to Canada (thank you, 78th Fraser Highlanders), and early accounts of the game are replete with references to Colonel Smith or Major Jones or the Commissioner of Police. When early regiments were disbanded in Canada, and their members given tracts of land, the regimental officers became the elite of the new community, and often formed the first curling clubs.

The association of curling with the military has continued to the present day. Most Canadian Forces Bases (CFBs), both at home and abroad, featured a curling club, particularly in the years following World War II. Those clubs catered to members of the Canadian Forces and also welcomed local residents to the sport. Curling in the Forces did several things, all of them good. The game was considered good for morale and fitness. In a service that required members to dine and socialize in certain strata (officers' mess, non-commissioned dining area), curling became a democratic "melting pot"—the colonel could play with, or against, the corporal; the pilot with the tank driver. In countries outside Canada, much of the growth of curling owes its development to Canadian Forces clubs. In Germany, for example, the residents of Lahr and Baden-Soellingen became enthusiastic members of the CFB curling clubs there. Those clubs in turn stimulated the development of German curling at the world level. Keith Wendorf, a Canadian who went to Germany to manage the Rhine Valley Curling Club in Lahr, turned it into a model club and also skipped Germany's national team to its best-ever Silver Broom finish, a silver medal, in 1983. When the base in Lahr

**Western Canada was famous for starting the carspiel, with four automobiles provided as the prize for the winners. Perhaps that was the impetus for the Rhine Valley Curling Club to provide bicycles for its four winners at the famed International Bonspiel in Lahr, Germany.**

*Photo by Keith Wendorf.*

was closed down, Wendorf became the national coach in Germany, and subsequently a development officer of the World Curling Federation.

Historians tell us that one of the main differences between the expansion to the West in Canada, compared with that of the United States, was the presence of the North West Mounted Police. In those early days, the scarlet-coated representatives of law and order were all-important figures in the growing communities. And it seemed that all of them were curlers, either before their arrival or shortly after.

An indication of their importance can be inferred from the story told by Laura Beatrice Berton in her book *I Married the Klondike*. At the turn of the twentieth century, Laura Thompson was a young kindergarten teacher who answered an advertisement for someone who could play the piano and sing, and teach the young children of Dawson. The promise of adventure in a far-off part of Canada caught her fancy, and she left her home in Ontario for the Yukon. It didn't take long for her to discover she loved the Klondike, and would spend the rest of her life there.

As a teacher and a musician, she moved in the best circles of Dawson society. In 1908, she accepted the invitation of the police commissioner and his wife to travel with them in an open police sleigh to Granville where the commissioner had been invited to officiate at the opening of a new curling rink. The fact that the opening would involve the police commissioner was an indication of his importance in the community, as well as the importance of curling. But this was no ordinary visit. The distance was 60 miles, and the journey would take two days and one night by horse and sleigh. The sub-zero weather did not deter the youthful Miss Thompson and, in Granville, after playing the piano and singing a number of songs, she was much in demand at the dance that followed. One of the young men who sought her attention was Frank Berton, who would later become her husband. Their first son, Pierre, is Canada's best-known writer of popular Canadian history.

A few years earlier, there was another momentous occasion in Canadian curling. It was in December of 1902 that a hearty group of 28 curlers arrived in Canada from Scotland. Disembarking in Halifax, they toured Atlantic Canada, moved on to Quebec and Ontario, and eventually arrived in Winnipeg on February 4, 1903. The touring captain, Rev. John Kerr, noted that, "if Canada be the chosen home of Scotland's ain game . . . then undoubtedly Winnipeg is the very fireplace or hearth of the game in the Dominion". After non-stop curling and banqueting there, they departed Winnipeg for games in Minneapolis-St. Paul. They then headed back east, with stops in the US, and back to Scotland. That first Scots tour of Canada is a separate story in itself (see chapter 6), and its impact is still being felt today.

Later in 1903, Major (later Colonel) Walker of the North West Mounted Police suggested the formation of a Western Curling Association, separate from the Manitoba and North West Curling Association, but the idea, presented some-what hastily at a bonspiel in Calgary, failed to gain acceptance. Undaunted, Major Walker tried again in 1904, and this time was successful. The Alberta Branch of the RCCC thus came into being.

Within five years of the Scots' visit, Canada returned the favour by sending a touring team to Scotland, where the Canadians won 23 of the 26 matches played. Following that visit, the Canadian team travelled to Switzerland for "some friendly games." These inter-country tours, inaugurated over a hundred years ago, still continue.

In 1906, the British Columbia branch of the RCCC was formed. And in the same year, Alberta and Saskatchewan held their first inter-provincial match, with Alberta emerging as winner.

In 1910, there was a major societal change that helped foster curling everywhere. Starting in the US, and then moving into Canada, the five-day work week was introduced, slowly at first, and then with growing prevalence. "The weekend," with all its implications for extended leisure pursuits, had arrived.

Of even greater importance to the growth of curling was the opening up of the western provinces with paved highways. In the first days of the game on the Prairies, small, one- and two-sheet clubs were built close to the players' homes. But as highways replaced dirt roads and cars became more common, it became ever easier for curlers to drive to a newer club with more sheets of ice where greater numbers could gather.

While Manitobans have long considered themselves to be in the centre of the curling universe (four national men's and women's titles in the decade 1993–2002 are powerful arguments), other provinces are ready to challenge their assertion. Alberta can also boast four national championships in the same period, while B.C., Saskatchewan, Ontario, and Nova Scotia claim three Brier and Hearts crowns each. Saskatchewan, however, trumps all the other provinces with the fact that, on April 24, 2002, the provincial legislature recognized curling as "the official sport of the province." Earlier Saskatchewan MPs and famous curlers, Bob (Peewee) Pickering, member from 1978 to 1991, and Rick Folk (1982 to 1986) are undoubtedly in favour of the designation.

There was nothing fancy about most clubs. What was important was the sense of belonging, of becoming involved in a game that attracted most members of the community. In his book *Saskatchewan Curling—Heartland Tradition*, Bill Argan tells of his own start in the game. The Regina club, he writes, was "halfway between home and band practice." We curled, he continued "on natural ice with colorless rings and unmatched rocks in a very cold rink" (vii).

As in eastern Canada, the curling club was more than just an athletic club. It became the social centre of the community, perhaps best exemplified by a short 1963 National Film Board movie, *Gone Curling*, which depicted a lone

**In April 1901, J. T. Lithgow played Col.
Rourke for the Dawson Curling Club
championship.**

*H.J. Goetzman photo from the University of
Washington collection (#3023), courtesy of
the Yukon Territorial Archives, #1213.*

visitor to a town, trying to find a variety of people, only to discover they had all
"gone curling."

The Canadian west, however, saw curling move from a purely merchant-
driven, elitist sport to a fully democratic one, earlier than in the east. Perhaps
an agrarian culture was more amenable to such a levelling of society than the
more staid and business-driven society of eastern Canada. Eventually, both parts
of the country would celebrate curling at a wide variety of levels. As Kerr reported in his book, which describes details of the Scots Tour, a toast in Hamilton
by Adam Brown, Postmaster-General, captured both the essence of the game and
its participants in the new country. Said Brown, "Worth, not birth, is an article
in the Scottish creed" (370). That feeling enveloped the game in Canada, more
and more, as the years sped by.

# CHAPTER 5

# Victoria's Influence: The Moral Imperative

**Any game, as it develops, is dependent on rules. Generally speaking, the rules** tell us how to play the game within the confines of accepted behaviour. Or, in the overworked phrase of today, how to compete on a "level playing field." By definition, playing outside the rules is considered cheating. But not always—not in all games. In baseball, for example, it is considered within the custom of the game to try and subtly persuade the umpire that a strike is really a ball. Or vice versa. The batter does so, and so does the catcher. It's an integral part of the game, and is considered not only acceptable, but also desirable.

Curling, too, has rules that govern the sport. In most cases the rules are technical, and detail the boundaries of the sport: measurements, what to do when something specific, or untoward, happens. Then there are rules that govern the behaviour of the players. In many cases these are dependent on the honour of the players involved—what has often been called "obedience to the unenforceable." One of the hallmarks of the game is the players' feeling, whether at the beginner stage or the elite level, that the honour of the game is sacrosanct. Most of the time, we take our cues for our conduct from the society in which we find ourselves.

In the case of curling, the central tenets of behaviour, both of yesterday and today, are derived from Victorian times. That was an era when team sports were becoming important, and when the rules for all sports were either being fashioned within the spectrum of chivalry, or recast in that mold. The earlier times of knighthood, King Arthur, Lancelot and the Round Table were brought into everyday living through the rules of each sport as Victorian gentlemen developed those games. Including curling.

Honour was the one absolute imperative. Of equal importance to the outcome of the game was the manner in which the game was played. No true gentleman cheated at curling, and that attitude still exists today.

In the rules of the World Curling Federation, there is a section entitled The Spirit of Curling. It says, in part, that "curlers play to win but never to humble their opponents. A true curler would prefer to lose rather than win unfairly." Vince Lombardi's dictum that "winning is the only thing" does not apply to curling. Nor does Leo Durocher's observation that "nice guys finish last."

In the Canadian Curling Association's rule book, there are two special sections that appear before any of the rules of the game are set out: the Curler's Code of Ethics, and a section on Fair Play. Both echo the Spirit of Curling from the WCF Rule Book.

"I will play the game with a spirit of good sportsmanship," says the Code of Ethics. "I will conduct myself in an honourable manner both on and off the ice," it continues, and goes on to say "I will take no action that could be interpreted as an attempt to intimidate or demean my opponents, teammates or officials."

There were other rules (no longer in use) in the early days of the game, that followed the same pattern of probity. For example, Rule 12 (from New Brunswick's early days) said that "if any player engaged, or belonging to either of the competing clubs, shall speak to, taunt or otherwise interrupt any other player, not of his own party, while preparing to play his stone, so as to disconcert him, one shot shall be added to the score of the party so interrupted, for each interruption, and play proceed."

The story of the Fergus curler who was fined for unbecoming conduct, profanity and a lack of respect for his teammates is one that has probably been

"Obedience to the unenforceable" is the phrase often used to describe the obligations—and rules—of curling. Take the example of a burned rock, a stone accidentally touched by the broom or brush of a sweeper, or by any of his or her equipment. The old rule called for the player who burned the stone to remove it immediately. Nowadays there are a variety of rules options available. But in the case of a touched stone, the central fact remains: it is up to the player involved to tell of the infraction. In almost every case, only the player involved knows if the stone has been touched, and the player is honour-bound to declare it. There may be no discernible sound of brush touching granite, no change in direction. The opposition may be unaware the stone has been burned. No official can call it. But the rule is quite explicit. The player who touched the stone is to declare it. In over fifty years of covering the sport, I cannot ever recall an instance when the player who committed the infraction, even if he or she was the only one who knew it, failed to mention the fact.

From whence came the phrase? Rushworth M. Kidder tells the story in his 1995 book *How Good People Make Tough Choices: Resolving the Dilemmas of Ethical Living*. Kidder reports that in 1924, *The Atlantic Monthly* published a verbatim record "by an accurate reporter" of a 1921 speech given in London by the eminent English jurist Lord Moulton.

In the course of his comments, Lord Moulton used the phrase to describe "the obedience of a man to that which he cannot be forced to obey. He is the enforcer of the law upon himself" (66–67).

Obedience to the unenforceable: it is a central tenet, the very foundation, of curling.

duplicated in clubs all across the land. Not all of them, subsequently, became an honorary member of the club, as happened in Fergus, but it is likely that they all accepted their punishment, in whatever form, as being a part of being a curler.

From whence came all this?

Mark Girouard, in his book *The Return to Camelot: Chivalry and the English Gentleman*, put it this way. "Chivalry helped to create the Victorian gentleman; and . . . the whole vast fabric of contemporary sport derives, not just from Victorian England, but from the small percentage of Victorian Englishmen who went to the public schools. The games which public school men took up or invented, the rules which they laid down for them, the clothes which they wore, the settings and equipment which they devised, the language which they used, and the seriousness with which they took the whole business gradually spread down the social scale and out to the rest of the world" (232).

Girouard noted that cricket, "often thought to be the most heroic and morally upright sport, in the late eighteenth century and early nineteenth century was anything but. At that time," he notes "the game was tied up with betting for high stakes, winning was all-important, matches were fixed by bribery or cunning, opposing sides not infrequently came to blows over a disputed decision, and the losing side tended to be beaten up by its infuriated supporters" (235).

Betting was also rife in Scottish curling in the late 1800s and early 1900s, and stories are still told of games being played for a year's wages. Obviously the loser's family suffered terribly. It was into this milieu that an aversion to gambling came into being. The Church, as might be expected, played a great part in helping to eliminate betting. In later years, the RCCC would declare that curling neither needed, nor wished to tolerate, gambling on the outcome of a game.

The concept of the chivalrous gentleman created a 180-degree change in cricket. And in other sports too. Nor was curling immune to these sea changes in Victorian society. Indeed, curling embraced the changes wholeheartedly. Victorian sportsmen, imbued with the concept of chivalry, applauded as the number of knights grew from 350 (at the start of Victoria's reign) to over 2,000 (at her death).

Curling in Scotland, which saw its greatest growth during Victoria's reign, was hardly immune to any of these influences, and became a part of the nobility of the day. It was in 1842 that the Earl of Mansfield, an enthusiastic curler, invited the Queen and Prince Albert to visit Scone Palace, his home outside Perth. There, on the polished hardwood floor of the long gallery, curling was demonstrated to the royal couple. And in a calculated move, the Prince consort was presented with a pair of silver-handled Ailsa Craig curling stones, and was invited to lend royal patronage to the sport. The following year, Queen Victoria granted permission to change the name of the Grand Caledonian Curling Club to the Royal Caledonian Curling Club. The RCCC, ever since, has been considered the Mother Club of curling worldwide, and the Victorian influence on the game was cemented by Mansfield's move. It was further re-enforced when a group of Scots curlers came to Canada in 1902, whose tour is worth a chapter all its own —see the next chapter.

Although he was not thinking of curling when he wrote his well-known lines, the famous American sportswriter Grantland Rice summed it up for many: "When the One Great Scorer comes to write against your name / He marks—not that you won or lost—but how you played the game."

In 1890, *Punch* magazine defined a sportsman as one who not only had become proficient in the practice of his sport, but someone who had learned

Whenever a Skins game is played, with a lot at stake, there's tension in the air. Skip Russ Howard (l) peeks around John Kawaja (of Ed Werenich's team), as Glenn Howard (rear) watches closely.

*Errol McGihon photo, courtesy McCain Foods (Canada).*

"to control his anger, to be considerate to his fellow men, to take no mean advantage, to resent as a dishonour the very suspicion of trickery, to bear aloft a cheerful countenance under disappointment, and never own himself defeated until the last breath is out of his body" (Girouard 235). Curlers, who might not phrase it quite the same way a century later, will nonetheless echo the sentiment.

But perhaps the most memorable description of sport of the time is in the poem that many young Canadian schoolchildren learned in their formative years—the one written by Sir Henry Newbolt (1862–1938), an Oxford lawyer, and later vice president of the Royal Society of Literature. Entitled "Vitai Lampada," the poem was as often as not declaimed by youthful students or Boy Scouts with all kinds of stirring accompaniment.

> There's a breathless hush in the Close tonight—
> Ten to make and the match to win—
> A bumping pitch and a blinding light,
> An hour to play and the last man in.
> And it's not for the sake of a ribboned coat
> Or the selfish hope of a season's fame,

But his Captain's hand on his shoulder smote;
"Play up! Play up! And play the game!"

The sand of the desert is sodden red—
Red with the wreck of a square that broke;
The Gatling's jammed and the colonel dead,
And the regiment's blind with dust and smoke,
The river of death has brimmed his banks,
And England's far and Honour a name,
But the voice of a schoolboy rallies the ranks,
"Play up! Play up! And play the game!"

This is the word that year by year,
While in her place the school is set,
Every one of her sons must hear,
And none that hears it dare forget.
This they all with a joyful mind,
Bear through life like a torch in flame,
And falling, fling to the host behind—
"Play up! Play up! And play the game!"
—1897

If the Victorian influence on curling was felt first in Scotland, then later in Canada and the United States, it made little headway in other curling nations, particularly in Europe. Scots curlers who helped start the game on the continent may have intoned their Victorian ideals of etiquette to newcomers to the game, along with directions on how to deliver a stone. Or they may not. Most Europeans considered such ideas to be more of a quaint British notion than an inherent part of their society or of curling as it developed there.

Almost a hundred years later, the shade of difference could be seen at the World Championship level. The year was 1983, the locale Regina, the event the

Paul Savage cradles the Air Canada
Silver Broom as the rest of the Ed
Werenich team receive their 1983 World
Championship gold medals in Regina.
The other members of the Toronto team
are (l-r) Neil Harrison, John Kawaja,
Savage, and Werenich. Silver medallist
Keith Wendorf looks on.
*Photo by Michael Burns.*

Air Canada Silver Broom. In those days (before the advent of time clocks), Ed
(the Wrench) Werenich, skip of the Canadian champions, had taken more time
than usual to decide on a shot against his Swedish opponent. As he was walking
down the ice to play his stone, the shot having been decided, he walked past
the Swedish third at the hog line, who was silently (and somewhat mockingly)
applauding the final decision by his opponent. A few paces later, Werenich realized
what he had seen, and it hit home. He stopped suddenly, wheeled around, and
advanced to his opponent. In unmistakable sign language he indicated his distaste
for such a breach, and graphically described what action he might take if it was
ever to be repeated.

**The handshake after the game—a Victorian vestige, or an essential part of curling? Wayne Sokolosky (Alberta) finished the 1976 Brier with six wins, four losses, while Jack MacDuff (Newfoundland) led his team to a satisfying Brier championship.**

*Photo by Michael Burns.*

While the Wrench was well known for his battles with authority off the ice, he was equally well known for his strict adherence to the rules and etiquette of the game, on the ice. He was not about to tolerate a mocking of that etiquette, even if it did occur in a world event. Although he would probably be the last person to think of himself as a Victorian, in his passion for curling, he echoed a Victorian respect for the game.

The most common aspect of that Victorian respect is the ritual handshake between players before and after each game. It is a vital element of curling that says, in gesture, we've agreed we'll play according to the rules, with dignity and honour. And afterward, thanks for the game.

CHAPTER 6

# The Scots Tour of 1902–03

**In today's world of instant everything, it's difficult to comprehend the amount** of time and effort and perseverance involved in arranging the first visit of Scots curlers to Canada and the USA.

In the early nineteenth century, Canadian curling still looked to Scotland for inspiration and support. So it was not surprising that the curlers in their new land would seek a visit from their peers in the old land. By the middle of the century, invitations had gone out to the home of the game for a group of Scots curlers to come over for a visit. That invitation of 1858 was repeated in 1870, 1874, and 1888. The 1874 invitation was carried to the annual meeting of the Royal Caledonian Curling Club personally by the chaplain of the Ontario Curling Association, later chaplain of the Canadian Branch, RCCC, the Rev. Dr. John Barclay. The visit would be promoted, not as a competition between countries, but as a friendly visit among Scots who also curled. However, little materialized from those early entreaties, other than a reply from a Sir William Elliot, in 1870, who indicated he would be happy to play any team in North America for a purse of 500 pounds sterling.

We have already seen the impact of gambling on curling in Scotland (see previous chapter) and the Church's attempt to snuff it out. So when Sir William's offer was reported to a convention of the Grand National Curling Club in the United States, the reply of one of the delegates was not entirely unexpected.

"A match for money," sniffed a Mr. Hoogland, "even though the sum be devoted to charity, would drag down curling to the level of baseball" (Kerr 5). Ouch.

Perhaps the "best fillip to the Scottish tour" wrote the Rev. John Kerr, curling historian and chaplain of the RCCC, was an article in *The Scotsman* newspaper of April 1902, in which the author, Hugh Cowan, described Winnipeg as "a curler's paradise." The article went on to say that if the tour could coincide with the annual Manitoba Bonspiel, then "I think I can promise the team such a welcome as they have never even dreamed of" (Kerr 5–6).

After some fifty years, the invitation was finally, and formally, accepted, and travel plans made. The Scots would curl in Halifax, Saint John, Quebec City, Montreal, Ottawa, Toronto (and seven other cities in Ontario), plus Detroit, before heading west to Winnipeg. From Winnipeg, the group would turn south, visit Minneapolis/St. Paul, en route to Chicago, Utica, and New York.

After departing Liverpool aboard the RMS *Bavarian* on December 18, 1902, the Scots arrived in Halifax on December 26 to start their tour. Not only in Halifax, but all across Canada and the States they discovered both the similarities—and differences—between the game in Scotland and Canada. "Not only were they curling morning, noon and night," reports John A. Stevenson in his book *Curling in Ontario*, "but they were overwhelmed by a rich variety of hospitalities and their powers of endurance became a byword" (101).

The Scots soon discovered just how different curling was in Canada. The majority of the visitors had never played indoors, nor had they ever used anything but a crampit from which to deliver their stones. At home, for the most part, they were only able to curl for a few weeks at a time, often on soft ice. In Canada, the season was prolonged, and the ice hard and keen. In addition, none had ever curled with irons, as they did in Quebec.

Stevenson, a transplanted Scot from Ayrshire, who was a correspondent for several newspapers (*London Times*, *Toronto Globe*, *Manchester Guardian*) was

The touring Scots team of 1902–03, photographed during their visit to Winnipeg.

*Bryants Studio, Winnipeg, National Archives of Canada, C-081312.*

just one who wrote about the tour. There were numerous newspaper and magazine articles written about the group wherever they travelled. They quickly became visiting celebrities, and when the tour was finished, the team captain, the Rev. John Kerr, penned a tome 787 pages in length. In it, he presented a detailed description of the games, the country, and indeed anything else that engaged the captain's mind. It is a veritable curling cornucopia of the time!

In those days, the only appropriate means of setting up the details of such a tour was either in person-to-person meetings, or by mail. Letters would travel by steamship or packet, and a reply could take weeks or months to arrive. Such a seemingly simple item as extending the visit in Ontario from nine days to thirteen, as requested by Ontario curlers, took an inordinate amount of time, ink, and perseverance.

It was obvious from the ambitious itinerary that the Scots thought the journey around North America would be not unlike a gentle tour around Scotland. Even though they may have misjudged the vast distances that would be covered, they were fully prepared for any eventuality. In a manner somewhat akin to today's Internet code-words, the outgoing Scots prepared a series of cable codes that could be used to cover almost any eventuality, particularly when every word on cable cost money!

For example, *Faro* meant, in cablese, "am out of funds, cable money care of, for sum of." Then there was *Isodynamic*, which, when attached to a curler's name, indicated "he is decidedly better and out of danger." What they hoped they wouldn't have to use was *Isboseth*, for the translation of that one meant the person mentioned alongside the term had died. And there were another forty-some code words, including *Cackle* (your cable has been received and understood), *Cave* (why do you not write?) and *Mabel* (what steamer are you returning by?)

Remember that life then proceeded at a more leisurely pace. Theirs was not a rapid journey: train speeds were about twenty miles per hour. There was time for banquets, speeches, and sightseeing in the new land. Then exactly two months later, after having travelled some 5,000 miles, having played 99 games (47 wins, 49 losses, and three ties), having dressed for numerous banquets, having downed countless drams and having sung—and resung—the same familiar songs, the group departed for home. On February 18, 1903, they left New York for Scotland, never having had occasion to cable Isboseth for any of their members. It is not known how many Faro cables were sent.

There were a number of long-lasting results of that two-month tour. Apart from the friendships created, there was the feeling that such visits should

**Canada's 1993 world winners in Geneva pose with the trophy. From l-r coach Larry Merkley, lead Peter Corner, second Wayne Middaugh, third Glenn Howard, and skip Russ Howard.**

*Photo courtesy* Canadian Curling News.

become a regular part of Canadian and Scottish curling life. There was also the feeling, on the part of the Scots, that they could no longer depend on natural ice for curling. Shortly after their return, the Scottish Ice Company was formed, and a six-sheet curling operation was built at Crossmyloof, three miles from the then heart of Glasgow, which provided a larger ice surface than the one they had enjoyed at the Granite Club in Toronto.

The only sour note of the Scots tour, reported John Stevenson (102–104), came via a sermon from a straitlaced Toronto cleric, one Rev. Dr. Milligan, who decried a Sunday trip by the visitors to Niagara Falls. "I had hoped for and had

**The Strathcona Cup comes out of storage every five years for the competition between Canada and Scotland.**

*Photo courtesy Royal Caledonian Curling Club.*

expected better than the spectacle of Scotsmen, with a minister at their head," he thundered from the pulpit, "on a Sunday jaunt to Niagara Falls." That was more than the Rev. John Kerr could take, and the day after Milligan's outburst had been reported in the Toronto paper, Kerr responded.

"I am sure," Kerr replied, in the forthright manner of many a Scot from then to now, "no one had any idea he would offend Dr. Milligan or anyone else by taking the opportunity . . . of visiting one of the most wonderful and awe-inspiring works of the Creator, whose majesty and glory are revealed in nature as well as in revelation, sometimes more attractively than in some of our churches, where 'new presbyter is but old priest writ large'". Nor could the doughty Dr. Kerr refrain from adding a poetic postscript to his published rejoinder. "The Reverend Doctor will pardon me," he concluded, "for transposing slightly a stanza from nature's great poet, Wordsworth, who was also a good Christian:

> One impulse from Niagara
> Will teach you more of man
> Of moral evil and of good
> Than Dr. Milligan."

The 1902–03 tour of Scots led to a return visit of Canadian curlers to Scotland in 1909. And once again, it was a Scottish-Canadian who put his name to one of the oldest curling trophies in history. His story, in far greater detail than can be given here, is that of a Canadian legend.

Donald Smith, at the age of 18, left his native Dufftown on the upper reaches of the River Spey to come to Canada in 1838. He started as a clerk with the Hudson's Bay Company and eventually rose to become its chief executive officer in Montreal. In 1871, he became a federal Member of Parliament. It was his recommendation that led to the formation of the North West Mounted Police, and as a founding member of the Canadian Pacific Railway, he risked his fortune during the five tumultuous years of its construction. In 1885, he drove the last spike in the transcontinental rail line that helped bind a new and young country together.

After returning to Britain, Smith was appointed to the House of Lords as Lord Strathcona and Mount Royal. In the years preceding 1909, when Strathcona was president of the Royal Caledonian Curling Club, he had commissioned a distinctive silver trophy to be created, and awarded originally to the losing Scots team of 1902–03. When the Canadian team of 1909 paid their first visit to Scotland, it was agreed that the trophy would henceforth be awarded to the winners. In 1909, it was Canada who took possession of the trophy.

Those first two visits—of Scots to Canada and Canadians to Scotland—started a tradition that continues to this day. The Strathcona Cup itself, however, is now so valuable that it is kept in Scotland for safe-keeping. But it does exist, unlike the mythical Ashes of cricket fame!

For some years, the to and fro of curlers from one curling bastion to the other was somewhat irregular. In later years, it became standardized so that Canadians would visit Scotland in years ending with an 8, while Scots would come to Canada in years that end with a 3. Of the eighteen visitations of inter-country play to date, Canada has won ten of the Strathcona Cup Matches, and Scotland eight.

The 2003 visit of a Scots team to Canada (half to play in western Canada; the other half in the east), marks the one hundredth anniversary of the initial Scots visit.

# CHAPTER 7

# Irons & Granites, Wooden Rocks, Jam Cans, and Thunder Mugs

**You would think that in a country as large, as geographically diverse, as steeped** in curling as Canada is, it would be a simple thing to produce superb curling stones for enthusiastic players. Right? Wrong.

Canada has tried time and again to produce curling stones to match those from Scotland. None have worked. Only in Scotland, you say? Well, not quite. In recent years, curling stones have been manufactured in Scotland, but the granite has been quarried in the Trefor Mountains of Wales. Still, many have asked why Canada, with at least half of it nestled in the Precambrian shield, and with its wealth of granite, with its million-plus curlers and over 1,300 clubs, has not been able to produce stones suitable for the game. From the Highlands of Cape Breton, through the Laurentians, the Niagara Escarpment, and the hard-rock mining areas of Northern Ontario and Quebec, to the rocky outcrops along the shoreline of Lake Superior, the search has been relentless. Farther west, Scots miners who emigrated to the interior of British Columbia in search of gold, also sought suitable granite for the game they brought with them. The search has proved elusive. Nowhere in this vast land, it seems, have curlers been able to find a granite that could be coaxed into the perfect curling stone.

**A mini-history of the curling stone: From channel stone, or loofies, and early Scottish stone (whatever size); to irons (c. Canada late 1800s to mid-1900s), and, finally, the standard granite of today.**

*Photo courtesy Scott Paper and Scott Tournament of Hearts.*

Not that there haven't been attempts. But every time a new source was teased into a curling stone, the crashing of stone upon stone would chip off shards of rock, or cracks would appear that would cause the stones to break apart.

In Canadian curling, incidentally, the words "rock" and "stone" are virtually interchangeable. "Last rock" is synonymous with "last stone." Not so in Scotland, where "stone" (or stane) is preferred to "rock." It's a subtle difference between the two curling bastions.

It seemed that nothing could be found to replace the granites from the island of Ailsa Craig, sometimes known as Paddy's Milestone, set in the Irish Sea off the Ayrshire coast of Scotland. Ailsa Craig granite is the hardest, purest, most dense granite extant. It is impervious to moisture, which in coarser granite freezes, expands, and "pops out" the impurities in the lesser stone, leaving it with an imperfect running surface.

Technically, Ailsa Craig is known as a volcanic plug, meaning the solidified lava in the vent of a long-ago volcano. It looms 1,100 feet [330 m] above the level of the surrounding ocean, and a fanciful story had it that the end of the world would have arrived when the island was reduced to a level stretch of rubble with heavy waves washing over it! The supply of raw material for curling stones seemed inexhaustible. But obtaining large enough "blanks" or "cheeses" from which a stone could be manufactured became an expensive process.

When it became clear that only one percent of all the rock blasted on the island produced cheeses large enough to make into a curling stone, the soaring costs dictated that the Ailsa quarry be closed down. In 1973, the island was

abandoned as the prime source of curling stones, and instead became a bird sanctuary. Ailsa granite, however, still comes into play today. The manufacturers have developed a method whereby a smaller piece of Ailsa granite can now be inserted into an older rock to provide the superior running surface of an Ailsa Craig. The "Ailsert" has arrived.

In the early game of curling, there were no specific dimensions for a curling stone, neither height nor weight nor diameter nor circumference. The early game was played with stones of varying sizes, shapes and weights—small ones that could skinny through a narrow port, huge ones that made a fantastic guard once in place, impossible to move. Shortly after the formation of the Grand Caledonian Curling Club in Scotland in 1838, there was a move toward standardization of stones. But even when the basic measurements were agreed upon, there was considerable controversy over the sole of the stone. And for some considerable time the matter of the running surface stirred much debate. Should it be flat? Concave? Convex? Which was best? Most predictable?

While it is as true today as it was long ago that the stones for the game all come from Scotland, there is still a Canadian connection, albeit little known, involving J.S. Russell. About this time, Mr. Russell, of Toronto, was an enthusiastic pillar of the curling community in early Ontario. A native of Lanarkshire in Scotland, Russell was secretary of the Ontario Curling Association from 1892 to 1902. He was also a later member of the famed Toronto Red Jackets foursome, and was always seeking a better, more predictable, curling stone. In the years after 1870, Russell experimented with a variety of running surfaces, and as

**One of the best known teams in the
period 1865–75 was the famous Toronto
Red Jackets, led by skip Capt. Charles
Perry. The team, shown in action on
Toronto Bay in this artist's rendition,
includes third David Walker, second
Thomas Gray, and lead Thomas McGaw.**
*Illustration courtesy Ontario Archives,
#S 837.*

curling moved indoors, with better and more stable ice conditions, the need for a standard stone became increasingly important. When he arrived at a design he deemed suitable, he passed along his suggestions to Andrew Kay in Scotland, the primary manufacturer of curling stones, and "Russell's Improved" stone, with its concave bottom and narrow running surface, became the standard around the world, and remains so to this day.

There were other Canadian contributions to alternative curling stones, although none were made as anything other than a short-term substitute for the real thing. The 78th Fraser Highlanders' idea of irons started out as a stop-gap measure that somehow turned into a long-term idea. Other concepts never became more than temporary: hardwood blocks of maple or birch, with angle-iron handles and iron striking bands; wooden blocks with holes filled with lead; why, there was even a suggestion that chamber pots (thunder mugs) might have been pulled out from under pioneer beds, filled with mortar and used for the occasional game! The mind boggles.

The use of irons in Quebec and eastern Ontario had a huge impact on the nature of the game. Both the weight and the texture of irons were such that even a heavy takeout shot, on target, would only move an iron a short distance, whereas the same weight of takeout, with a granite stone, would remove the stone completely. Thus a "granite-grade takeout" on a rock in front of the rings would, in irons play, turn into a raise! As a result, irons play was more amenable to a draw game (get a stone in the rings, then put up a guard), while the granite game became a takeout event. The takeout game is said to have originated and come into vogue with Winnipeg's famed Bob Dunbar rink around the end of the nineteenth century.

For younger curlers, the beauty of wooden stones was the fact that they could be fashioned to whatever weight was wanted. In more recent times, youngsters took a large marmalade or jam can, used a baseball bat to gently round out the bottom of the can, filled the can with cement, and put a U-shaped, tubular-steel handle, or an angle iron into the cement as it was setting. The resulting stones could be used in a backyard version of curling for youngsters on the days they weren't absorbed in hockey. According to some authorities,

**It was at the turn of the twentieth century that the game began to change. Bob Dunbar and his team from the Winnipeg Thistle Club were the ones who developed the takeout game to record their wins. The state of photography at the time (1899) could not capture action shots as today's photographers can. Instead they could pose—formally—for this photo.**

*Courtesy Western Canada Pictorial Index, #A0103-03192.*

jam-can curling got its start in 1946, when Harold Covell, a Regina school principal, came up with the idea and initiated his pupils into the enjoyment of the game.

Towards the end of the 1900s a variety of plastic "little rocks" were developed, which permitted pre-teens to learn proper delivery as a preliminary to using full-weight granites. Such modern-technology stones helped to initiate young curlers into the game when some of them were only slightly heavier than the granites their parents used.

As for granites? Actually, the stones of yesterday and today are, technically speaking, not granite at all. They are, say geologists, igneous rocks, composed of granite porphyry, in which orthoclase and plagioclase felspar are entwined with clear quartz. They were formed originally through the cooling of the magma that forms the earth's mantle.

But curlers not necessarily being geologists, simply call them granites. If that weren't so, think of how many "Granite Clubs" across the country would have to change their name! Somehow, it doesn't seem apt to think of going to the "Igneous Rock (and Felspar) Curling Club" for a Wednesday-night game.

Better stick with the Granite CC.

The other essential article in the game is the broom or brush. And what a change has occurred over the past half-century in that implement! In the beginning of the Canadian game, there were two major necessities: a shovel and a broom. Both were needed primarily to remove the snow and prepare the ice on the river or pond for play. Once that was done, the shovel could be set aside, but the broom was retained in case of falling or drifting snow. When curling moved indoors, the shovel became redundant, except for removing accumulated snow after scraping the ice.

Somewhere around the beginning of the twentieth century, when everyday house brooms were being used, there were those who suspected that vigourous sweeping could influence both the path and the distance a rock could travel.

Early experiments were conducted, using an inclined plane down which a rock could be slid. It was soon discovered that judicious sweeping could increase the distance a rock could travel by as much as 10 to 15 feet [3 to 4.5 m], depending on the condition of the ice surface. And every experiment since has proved the same thing: expert sweeping or brushing can produce winning shots.

The delivered stone does not travel in an arc, but in a straight line at first, and then, as its momentum decreases, the rotation of the rock takes effect. Knowledgeable sweepers not only can increase the distance a stone might travel, but can also delay the moment the stone begins to curl. Thus, sweeping both for "line" and "distance" became an essential part of the game.

What curling lore really needs right now is someone like Calgary journalist Bruce Dowbiggin, whose book, *The Stick*, details magnificently the development of the hockey stick. A similar book on "The Broom" would show the move from the Scottish broom "cowes" (bunches of broom twigs tied together) to the circular broom. About the time Scots were switching to the brush, curlers in Canada were using the unwieldy house broom. It wasn't long before they moved to the thinner, longer-strawed "buffalo" broom, and then to the paddle-like curling broom that captivated many a younger curler with its satisfying thwacking sound on the ice.

When, in 1958, Fern Marchessault of Montreal inverted the corn straw in the centre of the broom to form "the Blackjack," the result produced not only a deafening sound (much admired by muscular front-end sweepers; much maligned by elderly spectators), but also left considerable mounds of debris all over the ice that could affect the course of stones of both teams. "Keep it clean" became a watchword of sweepers in the heyday (hayday?) of the corn broom. Eventually, when Calgary curling developer Ted Thonger invented "the rink rat"—a synthetic, three-fingered broom—he boasted that there would be no more corn chaff on the ice, but did allow that there might be some fluff from the cotton that covered the springy pieces of plastic in the interior of the broom!

The Brier of 1977 was played in the Olympic Velodrome in Montreal. Here Ron Green and Reid Ferguson of Ontario wield their Rink Rat brooms to settle an Ontario stone into position.

*Photo by Michael Burns.*

The problem with all of these brooms was the damage the sweeping could inflict, partly to the ice, but, more importantly, to the hands of the players. Wielding such a broom over two or three 12-end games in a day, as in the Brier, left curlers with bleeding palms and calluses.

Then in the late sixties, a pair of Calgary curlers, John Mayer and Bruce Stewart, switched from a broom to the horsehair brush much favoured by Scots curlers. And soon discovered they could get the same results as the corn broom, but without the pain and blisters. It wasn't long before others joined the parade

**If sweeping didn't produce results, would these Quebec curlers have worked so hard? From l-r , Dan Lemery, Don Westphal, and Louis Biron work the brushes while Pierrre Charette shouts encouragement.**

*Photo by Michael Burns.*

—notably a youthful Paul Gowsell and his title-bound team of juniors—and a variety of brush heads were available: hog's hair, horsehair, and synthetic coverings in a bewildering set of coverings and styles, still in use today.

OK, we've covered stones and brooms: what else is left? Ice, naturally. And here we are getting out of the orbit of almost all curlers. While 98 percent of all curlers will pontificate about what it is that makes "good ice," 98 percent of all curlers haven't an ice-worm's idea of *why* it is good ice.

In the early days in both Scotland and Canada, ice was where you found it, and the way you found it was the way you played it. It was outdoors, of course, just the way nature prepared it, perhaps on a sluggish stream, a stretch of still water behind a dam, on a pond or lake. It had to be sufficiently thick—six to seven inches [15 to 17 cm]—to hold the assorted stones, curlers, and their provisions, when "brooms would be stacked." Andrew Bruce of Scotland, the Earl of Elgin and Kincardine, and a past president of the RCCC, likes to sing a song that suggests "five inches of ice is a boon beyond price and we'll all go a-curling today." Indeed, in the earliest days of the game, most local activity would stop while all gathered about the stretch of ice that beckoned the curlers. In those days getting a sufficient thickness of ice wasn't too difficult. But in later years, as climate change slowly set in, Scotland found it difficult to find six or seven inches of ice on which to hold their famed Grand Match (North of Scotland versus South). Indeed, the last time a Grand Match was held on outdoor ice in Scotland was in February 1979 on the lake of Menteith.

By 1837, Montreal curlers would have been well aware of John Cairnie's treatise on "artificial pond making." Cairnie, a Scottish doctor, was one of the most celebrated of Scots curlers and curling administrators, and is kept in Scottish curlers' memory through the use of his name as the headquarters of the RCCC, Cairnie House, in Edinburgh. Scots had long known that getting ice to freeze over deep water was harder than over shallow water. Scots curlers newly arrived in Canada also knew that unless they could build some kind of protection from the biting cold, it didn't matter how deep the water was. In 1837, the curlers of Ste. Anne de Bellevue built a curling shed, where water was poured onto wooden flooring and allowed to freeze. When covered over, it became the first indoor rink in Canada. Farther west, on the Prairies, hay or straw bales were used to provide shelter from the wind. The bales allowed the prairie cold to permeate the walls and aid in the freezing of the ice, but protected curlers from the ever-present wind. In the far north, there are stories of ice blocks being used in place of the hay bales to create a curling club—a club that melted in the spring, only to be reborn and rebuilt in the first frost of the fall.

As the country prospered and grew, so did curling. Some of the clubs that moved indoors stuck with natural ice, and though they may not have had to contend with wind and snow, curling conditions were often unpredictable. The weather outside affected the curling inside. But as refrigeration equipment became more easily obtainable, more economical, more and more clubs switched to the certainty—and longer season—provided by artificial ice.

With refrigeration, a whole new dimension of curling was possible. In particular, after World War II, there was a building boom that saw new clubs spring up like mushrooms after a warm rain. More attention was paid to the construction of the ice shed, and the curlers' demand for better ice. Contractors would excavate a depth below the frost line in which coarse gravel and sand could be poured to create a level area, free from frost heaving. Iron pipes, through which a refrigerant could flow, were laid on wooden sleepers, and sand covered all. Later the sand would give way to a cement floor, and eventually, a "floating cement" floor, meaning a concrete slab, with pipes embedded in it, would "float" on a layer of insulation. Then the ice-maker could work his magic. Pebbling the ice with a steaming spray of water created the knobby surface that permitted a stone to travel a much greater distance. In the days before pebbling cans, which were used to hold the hot water, some ice-makers used a length of perforated pipe attached to a hose, that could be dragged diagonally across the ice in one direction, and then another (at right angles to the first) to create a diamond pebble.

The quality of the water became paramount. Water that was high in alkali content would leave "greasy" patches where the impurities would not freeze at the same temperature as the water. Instead the impurities would migrate to the surface of the ice where they created problems for curlers who were unaccustomed to it. Later, engineers would develop de-ionizing processes that would create water more akin to distilled water in purity. This resulted in faster freezing times, less power used by ice-making machinery, better ice.

**Sandra Schmirler.**

*Photo by Michael Burns.*

Some ice-makers became known for making "fast" ice, others for straight ice, and still others for creating ice "with a good swing" in it. It was all part of the growing up of the game.

In earlier times, the condition of the ice was taken as a challenge to each team. The "runs and falls" in the ice were accepted as something a canny skip would discover before his or her opponent did, and win the game playing "the ice as it is, not what you think it should be," as one veteran skip put it. The idea of "negative" ice—in which a skip would call for a turn to the stone that would counteract the direction the stone wanted to take due to the condition of the ice—was one that has largely been lost in today's cosseted game.

One thing about today's ice: it may not be as haphazard in design as in yesteryear, but it does permit the making of today's incredibly precise shots, and the game is the richer for it.

# CHAPTER 8

# The Ever-Changing Rules, and Customs, of the Game

**No game is static, as far as its rules are concerned, whether those rules are** codified and written into handbooks, with multiple clauses and sub-clauses; or whether they are simple and easily understood. And if that applies to the written codes, what about the "the unwritten rules"—the etiquette of the game?

In recent years, as curling has spread around the world, there has been a move to simplify and standardize its rules. Consider the delivery of the stone. In the early days of the Canadian game, when a curler delivered the stone from the hack, there might have been a step or two after release, but there was no slide. Years would go by before some curlers found their swing momentum resulted in an involuntary slide from the hack rather than a few short steps. Some Canadians, in delivering the stone, might (wow) slide to the back of the rings. It wasn't long before some of the better curlers could reach the tee line. Ken Watson, originator of the "long slide," could glide comfortably to the front of the rings. And beyond. Soon it was the slide that captured the fancy of newcomers. The delivery might be somewhat wide, or narrow, of the broom, but, oh, how they could slide!

To produce a graceful slide, curlers took to many methods of improving their footwear. Liquid solder, seasoned leather, plastic milk carton sides—all were attempted. And to some degree, all worked. Then came Teflon, the red brick slider and as other, more improved materials surfaced, it soon became apparent that a curler could slide any distance he or she wanted.

Stan Austman of Saskatchewan, in 1954, did just that. In a Canadian School Championship game, Austman, with perfect balance, slid the length of the ice and deposited his stone on the button as he slid through the rings. Was this what the game would become? A sliding contest?

It didn't take long before curling's solons decreed that the hog line should be the stop sign for a delivery. But that edict was too easy—and failed. What did the rules-makers mean by "stop"? A slight revision to the rule dictated that the curler should come to a "complete stop" at the hog line. But what is a complete stop? Some curlers would release the stone before the hog line, then stand up, hop over the hog line and move back into their crouch delivery to let their momentum carry them as far as it could. They claimed that, yes, they had come to a complete stop—if only for the merest fraction of a second. It obeyed the letter of the law, but not the spirit. The creators of the "stop" rule were unsure what to do. So they moved to a rule that called for the stone to be released before the hog line. Who cared where your momentum took you, or how far you slid, as long as the stone had been released in time? Most thought that rule would suffice.

But then the debate shifted again. The rule, which called for the release to be clearly visible before the *front* edge of the rock had reached the hog line, was switched to one that dictated a clear release before the *back* edge of the rock cleared the line. That seemed to work for Canada, but the rest of the world was still working on the former rule, the front edge rule. When Canada's 2001 champion, Randy Ferbey, played in the Ford World Championships in Lausanne, Switzerland, he ran into trouble. Ferbey, a noted long slider who often flirted with the hog line, was called for a delivery violation just once in the first nine games of round-robin play. But in his semifinal game against Switzerland, he was called three times. In the entire history of world play, it marked the first time

a player had been sanctioned that often in a single game. As might be imagined, tempers became frayed.

"By the way," you ask, "What is the origin of the term 'hog line'?" It's a question often asked but seldom answered, other than with a "beats-me" shrug of the shoulders.

According to Scots curlers, the term is derived from Scottish agriculture. In a country where so many sheep were raised, a lamb in its first year of life was called "a hog." (Don't ask.) In time, the name came to represent a straggler, a weakling, the one most likely to fall prey to predators, or to be culled from the flock. Similarly, a stone that could barely make it into the playing area was called a hog, and was therefore culled from the rest. The demarcation point to decide

which stone was alive and healthy and which was not was called the hog line. Originally, the hog line had only one use: to determine whether a stone was in play or not. It was only when the long slide came into the game that the near hog line came into use. In order to dissuade a generation of Stan Austman slide-alikes, it was agreed that there had to be a point where the handle of the stone should be released. And since the hog line was already there, why not use it as the demarcation point? The difficulty, of course, came when someone had to judge whether the release of the stone had been made before reaching the hog line, or after. Was the stone a sickly lamb, or healthy ram? Ewe decide (ouch), said the curlers, and if you break the hog-line rule you take the stone off.

The next move, still in the preliminary stage in 2002, would be the development of an electronic hog-line sensor that could make calling a hog-line infraction an objective, mechanical matter, rather than a subjective, open-to-criticism call.

And that was just one rule.

The attempt to find common ground in international rules has been an on-again, off-again affair. After a short flurry of activity at the start of the Scotch Cup, there was a period when the rules changed very little. In 1971, a few years after the advent of the Air Canada Silver Broom, the International Curling Federation agreed that it would be "a good thing" to try to standardize the rules of curling for all countries. At that time, although most rules in the major countries were essentially the same, there were slight variations among Canada, the United States, Scotland, and Europe. The ICF enlisted the support of Lachlan "Duke" McTavish of Toronto to work on the proposals. McTavish, a lawyer and ardent curler, was a past president of the Ontario Curling Association, and was also legal counsel to the Government of Ontario. That meant it was his job to put into proper and unambiguous language the new laws being created by Parliament. He had even written a textbook on the grammar and linguistic construction of rules and laws. But even with so erudite and knowledgeable a person, the task of creating an international curling rule book proved difficult. While he was able to produce a set of rules that appeared universally acceptable and in keeping with the history and philosophy of curling, there were still some sections of the rule book that defied agreement.

Even such a simple rule as the dimensions of a sheet of ice caused problems. In the early days of the game, both in Scotland and Canada, there was no specified width to the playing area. Or length, for that matter. If outdoor conditions were not suitable (heavy ice, or falling snow), and it was mutually agreed, the length of the ice could be shortened. If there was a slant or fall in the ice, you simply used as much ice as was required to play the game. Width didn't matter. When curling moved indoors, however, a finite length and width had to be decided, for obvious construction reasons. The length of a sheet of ice was

easily determined. But to build a clear span of roof over a width of two, four, or six sheets of ice required more precise mathematics. So the width of a sheet of indoor ice was mandated at 14 feet, 2 inches [4.31 m]—just wide enough to allow a stone to stop on the tee line on either side of the ice, barely outside the 12-foot ring, but not touching the side boards or side line. Twelve feet, plus one stone's width on either side of the rings, plus a bit "of air," and voilá, 14 feet, 2 inches. Simple, yes? Well, no.

When it came time for world play, Europeans questioned the Canadian width. It wasn't long before they convinced the Canadians that a stone on the tee line, barely biting the 12-foot circle, should be able to be missed, *on either side of the stone*, the same as a stone in the centre of the playing area. So the width for international play became 15 feet, 7 inches [4.75 m]. Or, two stones' width on either side of the 12-foot ring. OK? OK.

Obviously, however, it would be impossible to legislate that width for clubs that had already been built, based on the Canadian width of 14 feet, 2 inches.

The rules grew out of the game, as played in Scotland, and in Canada. In the early days of curling in Canada, it was natural that players would emulate the game they had left behind in Scotland. But it wasn't long before Canada's climate had its impact on how curling should be played—and on the rules. Canada and Scotland soon reached a fork in the road when it came to the direction curling would take. Was it Yogi Berra who said, many years later, "When you come to a fork in the road, take it"? That's what Canada and Scotland did. As much as anything else, it was the temperature in each country that dictated the direction to be taken.

For example, the ice on Scottish ponds, lochs, and rivers was not nearly as thick as the ice covering Canadian lakes and ponds. So there was no problem for early Canadian curlers to "hack out" a foothold in the ice, which would give them a secure starting point for the stone's delivery. In Scotland, where the ice was seldom thicker than three to five inches, curlers risked an early (and cold) bath if they tried to chip out a two- or three-inch foothold.

So in Scotland, early curlers opted for devices, called trickers or cramps, that attached to the feet to provide a secure footing on the ice; or "crampits," from which a curler delivered the stone. The crampit (sometimes called a foot-iron) was a flat metal plate, 12–14 inches [30–35 cm] in width and a yard [metre] in length. It was placed securely on the ice and, by putting his foot against a raised metal ridge at the back of the crampit, the curler was able to stand securely, and then with a pendulum swing, deliver the stone towards its mark. There was no slide. The crampit remained standard in Scotland for many curlers until just after World War II.

The first Scotch Cup was the catalyst in starting the move to standardization of rules. Before the Richardsons of Canada could take on the Scots, agreement had to be reached concerning the use of the crampit (for Scotsman Willie Young) and the use of the Canadian hack (for Ernie Richardson's foursome). The length of the slide in delivering the stone had to be agreed upon.

Ken Watson, the Canadian most heavily involved in the Scotch Cup, was no stranger to the rules, or to amicable discussions aimed at finding common ground. As the first three-time Brier champion, a former schoolteacher and key person in the establishment of the Canadian School Curling Championships, Watson had the prestige and stature, and the easy authority to help settle differences. He did so smoothly and with remarkably little fuss. The most contentious issues were soon cleared away and other, less vital rules were quickly agreed upon.

When Scotland moved from the crampit to the hack, it was a different kind of hack from Canada's. Because many of Scotland's ice rinks also featured skating, it was necessary to have hacks that could be removed quickly when it was time for the skaters to come on the ice. So the Scottish hack was not like Canada's permanently positioned, sunken hack. In fact, Scotland used either of two hacks. The first (used in the early Scotch Cups) was a rubber-coated piece of rectangular wood, angled at the front, that sat on top of the ice (by two or three inches) and was held in position with four pins, one at each of the four corners. There was only one hack at either end of the ice, and if a left-handed curler wanted to use the hack, it would be lifted out of its pin placement and moved to the pin holes on the other side of the centre line. Occasionally, as the holes became larger, the hack would slip out of the pin holes and provide a surprise ending to the delivery.

The Scots also used another form of hack that was almost as insecure as the angled wood and rubber one. This was a flat, H-shaped piece of metal, like an oversized belt buckle. The cross bar of the letter was perpendicular to the flat sides of the H, and was raised about an inch above the ice. Once again there were four pins at the top and bottom of each upright part of the H. These pins were inserted into the ice, and the player placed his foot against the upright bar, usually with a glove placed over the bar for added purchase. As with the wood and rubber hack, it too had to be available for placement on either side of the centre line, so there was always the danger of slipping. Indeed, each delivery for the visiting Canadians became an adventure.

The sunken, permanent Canadian hack, on the other hand, provided a more secure foothold for delivery. But it was something more. It changed the delivery motion drastically from the Scots' crampit delivery. The crampit called for a

**Two of Canada's modern-era greats, Wayne Middaugh and Kevin Martin, share a relaxed moment during a Skins game.**

*Errol McGihon photo courtesy McCain Foods (Canada).*

curler to keep his shoulders and hips lined up along the line of delivery. The stone was swung across the body, and there was little or no follow-through. The Canadian delivery, in contrast, called for the curler to sit in the hack with his body and shoulders at right angles to the line of delivery. In the Canadian game, the hack foot was in line with the stone's direction, while the other foot could follow through, behind the stone, along the same line of delivery. Eventually, what started as a follow-through of a few steps became a short slide (to the back of the rings), and then longer (to the tee line) and longer (the front rings) and still longer (the hog line).

Even NASA contributed to curling and its rules. When the space program needed a material that would provide a friction-free covering for the nose cone of rockets and spacecraft returning to earth, Teflon was born. With Teflon (and its successors) on the sole of the sliding shoe, a curler could now glide effortlessly along the ice.

The grace, elegance, and balletic beauty of the delivery became a given in the game, except that now the rules had to be changed to limit the length of the slide. The first hog-line infraction was now possible.

Years later, new rules would be constructed to help improve the game. There was a move in 1989, dictated by necessity, that saw time clocks introduced to curling. That was the year the ICF moved to integrate the Women's World Championship with the Men's, in Milwaukee. With this doubling of game activity, the worry for the organizers was that games could drag on to unmanageable lengths. The solution? Time clocks.

The original research on time clocks had started in 1983, and when The Sports Network (TSN) introduced time clocks to curling's Skins Game in 1986, they proved a popular addition to the game, in that the clock mandated a specific length of time for each team's game. When the Milwaukee organizers, in 1989, became concerned about scheduling four or five draws a day, the time clock turned out to be the saving grace of the event. Time clocks have been present in top-level curling ever since.

The "Free Guard Zone" rule arrived two years later, as a modification to a 1991 big-money competition, The Moncton 100. The event was designed as a celebration of Moncton's civic centennial, and with $250,000 in prize money, it was the world's richest cashspiel. To give the event added allure, one of the competing teams, Ontario's Russ Howard foursome, suggested a rule change similar to one of his team's practice drills: neither side would be allowed to remove the first four stones of an end from play, whether in the rings or not. They could move the rocks around, but not remove them. The rule, dubbed The Howard Rule, proved a popular addition to the Moncton event. A year later, when renamed the Free Guard Zone rule, and with one modification, it became a feature of the Winter Olympics of 1992. The Olympic modification restricted the Free Guard Zone to an area between the hog line and the tee line *outside the rings*. While subsequently Canada opted for a three-rock FGZ rule, the rest of the world thought a four-rock rule was preferable.

By the turn of the twenty-first century, the World Curling Federation began again to contemplate the standardization of the rules.

While the effort to provide standard rules has been mostly successful, it has not been possible to reach agreement on all regulations. For whatever reason, it has not been possible to gain agreement between the minority of curlers in the world (as represented by the smaller nations of the WCF) and the majority, as represented by the Canadian Curling Association, on certain other rules. Rules such as sweeping behind the tee line (who and how many), the Free Guard Zone (three or four rocks), and when a stone is in hog-line violation (when it reaches

the hog line, or when it crosses it), are but three of the rules still awaiting world-wide agreement. But don't despair, agreement will come.

Go back in time—way back—and you can get a perfect example of the divisiveness of a rules debate that raises nary an eyebrow now. Curlers take it for granted that there has always been an in-turn and an out-turn in the delivery of the stone. Not so. In the Scotland of the late 1700s, curlers simply threw their stones up and down the ice. Straight handle, no turn. Then the curlers in the parish of Fenwick (pronounced *Fen-ick*) discovered that if you imparted a turn, or as they called it, a twist, to the handle in delivery, their stone would curl around an opposition rock and be hidden.

The uproar that ensued over this "illegal" method of play threatened to split the game apart. "Tha's nae curling," some said. A few curlers of the day called for the twist to be outlawed as going against the spirit of the game. Curling, they said, wanted, and needed, straight shooters. Others reasoned that if the Fenwick curlers could make one stone curl around another and bury in behind a guard, then they could learn the same "illegal" manoeuvre for themselves, and beat the Fenwickians at their own game. And so the in-hand (in-turn) and out-hand (out-turn) came into being. According to some authorities, the curl in curling didn't come to Canada until somewhere around 1840. Up until then the stone was delivered with a (mostly) straight handle.

Before leaving this discussion, let us acknowledge the most solid thing about the rules of curling, and give thanks to the early Scots who promulgated them. Unlike so many other sports, which have developed the rules into clauses and subclauses, with arcane minutiae, where players try to find ways to circumvent the rules, curlers have prided themselves that they practise "obedience to the unenforceable." In short, they police themselves. Burn a rock? The etiquette of the game demands that the sweeper who does so is the one to remove the stone. In the case of the contentious hog-line rule, several provincial associations today have removed the hog-line officials and shunted them into the stands. They have found, as the early Scots could have told them, that players, when left to themselves, can police themselves perfectly well, without any adverse effect on the game.

Each year the changes continue, as they have since curlers started to create the perimeter of rules that surround the sport. For example, in October 1906, at the semi-annual meeting of the Ontario Curling Association, the sweeping rule was amended to read that a front line should be drawn "in front of and touching the outer ring of the head and no other player than skip or vice-skip, acting as a skip, shall sweep a stone after it has passed the front line." In other words, no front end sweepers in the house. That same year, it was agreed to limit the length of a (competitive) game to 18 ends, except for special competitions, in which case a game would be 22 ends. (Note that in New Zealand today, games are generally 21 ends long, as was the case in Scotland years before.)

But even at 22 ends, the game had been shortened. In early records, it was noted that a game could be of indeterminate length—the first team to record 31 points, no matter how long it took, would be the winner. From 22 ends, the march toward shorter games has been inexorable. Eighteen ends gave way to 16 ends and 14 ends—the latter length was used in the first year of the Brier, in 1927. Within a year, that had been reduced to 12 ends, and the 12-end games lasted till the 1977 Brier, when a championship game was reduced to 10 ends. In 1999, there was a move by the WCF to move championship games to 8 ends, a move that was defeated largely on the basis of a spirited defence of the status quo by Canadian officials, led by CCA president Jack Boutilier and General Manager Dave Parkes.

But with all the changes that have taken place over the years, curling is still a game with the fewest of rules possible; it is still a game that depends on the players themselves to follow the rules, both written and unwritten.

CHAPTER 9

# Birth of the Brier

**Although the name The Roaring Twenties had nothing to do with curling, it could** have. As Canada began its long recovery from the haunting horrors of the Great War, as it moved from economic distress to staid society and then to the flapper era, curling began its expansion into becoming a national sport. The Roaring Twenties loved the roaring game.

By now Winnipeg had established itself as the centre of curling, nationally. The annual Manitoba Bonspiel became the dominant event of the sport, and one company, the W. C. Macdonald Tobacco Company of Montreal, became a major benefactor and catalyst of the game.

In 1924, George J. Cameron, an enthusiastic Winnipeg curler, dreamed aloud his idea of uniting the east and west of Canada through curling. Cameron was president of W. L. Mackenzie and Company, the western representative of the Macdonald Tobacco Company since 1880. Two of his friends, Walter Payne, known as Manitoba's "thane of curling," and John T. Haig, a past president of the Manitoba Curling Association, encouraged his thinking. On his next trip to Montreal he placed his idea before the tobacco company. His proposal to cement the two islands of curling—east and west, irons and granites—was accepted by the company. While the theory was easily agreed, translating theory into practice was another matter altogether.

Curling in the west was essentially played with granite stones. In Montreal and Quebec City, irons play was favoured. Most of Ontario and Atlantic Canada were granite bastions, although irons still held sway in the Ottawa Valley and eastern Ontario. Both camps were adamant that their game was better. Getting the two to unite was almost impossible. But the granite group held the hammer, in the person of T. Howard Stewart of the Macdonald Company. Stewart, the brother of company president Walter Stewart (and uncle of David M. Stewart) was a granite enthusiast. Whether it was his influence or not, it is certain he was in favour of the rule, established at the beginning of the Brier, that granites only would be used in the new national competition.

The Macdonald Company agreed to support the establishment of the Macdonald Brier trophy, as a key part of the 1925 Manitoba Bonspiel. In addition to receiving the honour of having their names engraved on a magnificent silver trophy (later rechristened the British Consols trophy) the winners would receive an all-expense trip to eastern Canada for a series of friendly games against eastern teams. In 1925, the winner was Howard Wood of Winnipeg, whose rink of Johnny Erzinger, Vic Wood (brother) and Lionel Wood (son) travelled east in the spring of 1925.

However, there were two major problems with the trip. First of all, the weather failed to co-operate, and many games had to be cancelled when the natural ice turned soft. Secondly, George Cameron, who accompanied the "Pappy" Wood team, quickly realized that without the adrenalin of competition, the trip would be of little consequence.

In 1926, the winners of the Macdonald Trophy event—the George Sherwood rink—were sent east to participate in the famed Quebec Bonspiel, where they won the Holt Renfrew Trophy. This second visit attracted greater attention, and

There was only one team from the West at the inaugural Macdonald Brier at the Granite Club in Toronto—the Ossie Barkwell foursome from Yellow Grass, Saskatchewan. The 1927 competitors were (l-r) Pete Wilkin (third), Alf Hill (lead), Hector Hay (second), and Ossie Barkwell (skip). Note the circles on the ice, not painted.

*Photo courtesy Saskatchewan Sports Hall of Fame and Museum.*

subsequent conversations between Cameron and Thomas Rennie of Toronto (and others) led to the concept of a national event, with inaugural play to be held at the Granite Club in Toronto in 1927.

And so the Brier (a Macdonald Tobacco trademark name) as the national curling championship of Canada, was born.

Eight teams took part that first year. There was one rink from western Canada, skipped by Ossie Barkwell of Yellow Grass, Saskatchewan. There were provincial teams from Nova Scotia, New Brunswick, Quebec, and Ontario. City champions from Toronto and Montreal were on hand, plus an eighth team from Northern Ontario. Earlier it had been agreed that the fairest method of determining a winner was for each team to play each of the others—a round-robin series. The only time a playoff would be needed would be if two or more teams tied for first place.

**The first Brier winners in 1927 came from Nova Scotia. (l-r) Murray Macneill, Al MacInnes, Cliff Torey, Jim Donahue.**
*Courtesy Western Canada Pictorial Index, #A0306-09761.*

There has always been a question of why Ontario was allowed to have two entries, one from the southern part of the province, and one from the northern climes. No one seems to know the true reason, and those who might know are all dead. The phrase used often in curling, "lost in the mists of time," seems appropriate. The generally accepted notion is that when the event was being established, it was agreed that having an odd number of teams would be unwieldy. In later years, when it was suggested that the Northern Ontario entry be dropped, the reply from David M. Stewart was, "When you invite someone into your living room, you don't invite them to leave just because the numbers aren't right."

And so, Northern Ontario, with its four regional associations and its curlers stretched over a vast distance, remains a vital part of the Brier to this day.

One of the teams seeking the inaugural title was a Montreal rink skipped by Peter Lyall, with T. Howard Stewart playing second. Stewart would later compete in the 1932 Lake Placid Olympics; Lyall would become one of the first three trustees of the Brier, along with Thomas Rennie of Toronto, as Chairman, and Senator John T. Haig of Winnipeg.

The first winner was a foursome from Halifax, skipped by Professor Murray Macneill. When Macneill's original Nova Scotian team was unable to travel, he recruited three other skips to join him. The move paid off as Macneill, Al MacInnes, Cliff Torey, and Jim Donahue finished the round-robin series with six wins and only one loss. It is now a part of Brier lore that the Atlantic Canada quartet of four skips who won that first Brier never played together as a team again.

Games were 14 ends in length that first year, but were reduced to 12 ends for the 1928 event. The 12-end game was the norm until 1977, when games were shortened to 10 ends. And regardless of the score, it was a Brier rule that all games had to be played to completion of the allotted number of ends. Conceding a game that was beyond redemption was not allowed until 1973.

In 1928, it was decided to expand the event to ten teams, with the addition of two more teams from the West, and in 1932, city teams were discontinued, bringing the number of competing teams back to eight. In 1936, with the inclusion of British Columbia and Prince Edward Island, the number of competing entries returned to ten. Newfoundland entered the fray in 1951, and in 1975 a combined entry from Yukon and the Northwest Territories brought the total number of teams to 12, its current number.

In 1928, the Gordon Hudson rink from Manitoba, with Sam Penwarden, Ron Singbusch, and Bill Grant, finished the round-robin series in a three-way tie for first place with a 7-2 record. Two playoff wins gave Hudson the national title. The following year, when he was invited to return as defending champion, he repeated his victory with an unbeaten 9-0 record. There was one change in his team. Don Rollo played third, replacing Penwarden, who had died in the interim. Seventy-two years later, a gold heart-shaped pin, with Rollo's name on it, was discovered in the recesses of the Calgary Curling Club Hall of Fame, in the

It was Gordon Hudson of Winnipeg who began Manitoba's pre-eminence at the Brier. In 1929, with only one change in line-up (Don Rollo replaced Sam Penwarden, who had died that year), Hudson won his second national championship. From l-r, Hudson, Bill Grant (lead), Rollo (third), and Ron Singbusch.
*Photo courtesy Western Canada Pictorial Index A0103-03185.*

process of the research for this book. As the book went to press, arrangements were being made to send the pin to the Manitoba Curling Hall of Fame and Museum in Winnipeg.

The Brier continued to be played at the Granite Club in Toronto until 1940, when action was shifted to the Amphitheatre in Winnipeg. For the first time, matched stones, with coloured tops (for easier identification), were used, and a movie of the event was made. Play continued into the early forties, but from 1943–45, World War II travel restrictions forced a halt to Brier play.

A by-product of the Brier was the camaraderie established among curlers from the various provinces. The competition among the regions of the country echoed the early days of the game, when one town would compete against another. And, in the early days of the championship, the annual cross-Canada trek by train produced its own society. By the time the Brier trains (one from the east and one from the west) had rolled into the host community, the players had become well-acquainted. In spite of Mr. Kipling's decree, the twains of east and west did manage to meet, and the Brier became the model of bringing all parts of the country together. When air travel entered the picture, those early train-fed friendships (and hijinks) disappeared.

FOURTEENTH ANNUAL
MACDONALD'S BRIER TANKARD
DOMINION CURLING CHAMPIONSHIP
WINNIPEG, MANITOBA, MARCH 1940

David M. Stewart, the scion of the sponsoring family, and its public face at the Brier, was a Canadian history enthusiast who made sure that every provincial capital hosted the Brier at least once. His annual speech at the Tuesday evening banquet painted his enthusiasm for Canada and its history in bold strokes of passion and fervour. The Brier, according to David Stewart (whose coonskin coat became as much a symbol of the event as the purple heart) was pure Canadiana, and he revelled in it.

From the start of the Brier, it was apparent that a national body was needed to co-ordinate curling activity in the country. That body, the Dominion Curling

**When the Macdonald Brier came to Calgary in 1948, the pre-event parade was big news. And obviously it was chilly on the wagon carrying the Brier officials and trustees.**

*Photo by E.W. Cadman, Oliver Studios, courtesy of the Calgary Curling Hall of Fame.*

Association, was formed on March 6, 1935, with Senator John T. Haig as first president. In 1967, the DCA changed its name to the Canadian Curling Association. In 1990, the Canadian Ladies' Curling Association, which was formed in 1960, amalgamated with the (men's) association to form the new CCA (men and women).

During the initial decades of its existence, the Brier was known mainly just to curlers. But in the years after World War II, the event took a quantum leap in the eyes of the public, and it soon became as important a national—and public—event as the Stanley Cup or Grey Cup. Two reasons stand out for the transformation. The first was the involvement of a pair of advertising and public relations executives, Reg Geary and Frank O'Brien of Montreal. As employees of

In 1948, Reg Geary convinced the CBC to produce live radio coverage of the Macdonald Brier, with Vancouver's Bill Good (l) and Doug Smith of Montreal (r) providing the commentary. The move helped to make the Brier a "big-time" event.

*Photo courtesy* Canadian Curling News.

the tobacco company's advertising agency, they were given the task of making the Brier into a major event in the Canadian sporting parade. They did so by enlisting the help of the media, who found ideal working conditions when they arrived at each Brier site. And through the radio broadcasts, newspaper stories, and photographs, the public soon found the daily reports, akin to a soap opera, to their liking.

The second reason grew out of the first. In 1946, Geary convinced the CBC to provide full-network, live radio coverage of the Brier in Saskatoon. It fell to Doug Smith of Montreal and "Breathless" Bill Good of Winnipeg (later Vancouver) to provide the commentary. As luck would have it, the competition that year ended in a three-way tie, involving Alberta (Billy Rose), Manitoba (Leo Johnson), and Northern Ontario (Tom Ramsay). Good and Smith brought the full drama of each day's games, and then the play-offs (Rose won), to every corner of the country. Suddenly newspapers everywhere, in an attempt to match the radio reports, kept asking for stories on "that crazy curling thing going on in Saskatoon." Each succeeding year, the thirst for coverage escalated. Much of the credit for that is due to Frank O'Brien, the unfailingly good-natured and highly capable PR man.

When television came to the party, suddenly people at home were able to watch their heroes in action, and they loved it. The ratings increased year by year and, today, the Brier is one of the most avidly watched sporting events in Canada. At first, the coverage consisted of a daily half-hour report late at night. In 1962, on the spur of the moment, the CBC provided live coverage of the final playoff game between Ernie Richardson and Hector Gervais. In 1973, the CBC decided to move to scheduled live coverage of the final draw. The move backfired. The network had scheduled such coverage, convinced that the final round of games would determine the Brier champion, as had happened in most years. That year, however, Harvey Mazinke's Regina foursome so dominated the Brier that they clinched the title the night before the final draw. The Friday games turned out to be meaningless, but even so were given the full majesty of live television coverage! Today, between CBC and TSN, over fifty hours of live Brier coverage each year have helped to create a loyal and enthusiastic audience of curlers and non-curlers alike. Not only do viewers appreciate the grace and style of the curlers and their incredible shot-making abilities, but they find that the game is also peculiarly suited to television's demands.

In 1977, fifty years after the first Brier, the Macdonald Tobacco Company announced that it would discontinue its support of the Brier (it always disdained the term "sponsorship") in 1979. That year, with the playing of the final Macdonald Brier in Ottawa, there was an electric moment when every living Brier Championship skip was introduced and honoured. It was a moment of spell-binding curling history, and the photo of the event showcased the Brier in a distinct and compelling way. The Brier had become one of the jewels of the Canadian sporting scene, a jewel that has been polished in several excellent books about the event.

A five-man committee was named by the CCA to find a new sponsor. Led by former CCA president Clif Thompson, the committee (Harvey Mazinke, Frank Stent, Don Anderson, and Doug Maxwell) worked diligently to find a replacement for the Macdonald Company. After negotiations that required the CCA to change

**The fact that every living Brier winner was on hand for the fiftieth anniversary championship in Ottawa is ample indication of the esteem in which the Macdonald Brier was held. Back row (l-r) are Don Duguid, Orest Meleschuk, Harvey Mazinke, Bill Tetley, Jack MacDuff, Jim Ursel, Ed Lukowich, Barry Fry. Middle row (l-r) are Don Oyler, Matt Baldwin, Garnet Campbell, Ernie Richardson, Hector Gervais, Terry Braunstein, Ron Northcott, Alf Phillips Jr. Seated (l-r) are Gordon Campbell, Ken Watson, Ab Gowanlock, Billy Rose, Jimmy Welsh, Frenchy D'Amour, and Tom Ramsay.**

*Photo by Michael Burns.*

some of its preconditions, the committee was successful in attracting the support of the Labatt Brewing Company. The name "Brier" however, was the property of Macdonald's, and before they agreed to give permission for its continued use as the revered name of the Canadian Championship, they asked for, and received, agreement that the Brier name would never be used for commercial purposes. So if you ever wondered why there was never a Brier beer, now you know.

The first Labatt Brier took place in Calgary in 1980, and featured a major change in the event. Up to that point, the only time there had been playoffs was when two or three teams were tied for the top after the round-robin series. But television revels in playoffs and, in 1980, the Brier moved to a playoff format following the preliminary round-robin games.

Brewery sponsorships normally have a relatively short life, but the Labatt sponsorship of the Brier lasted 20 years, well past the norm. Finally, the suds support ran its course, and at the turn of the century, the Canadian arm of the giant Finnish telecommunications company, Nokia, took over.

The Brier, it must be noted, is far more than the Canadian Men's Curling Championship. In its early days, it was the catalyst for change in Canadian curling. The bitter rivalry between the apostles of irons curling and the disciples of the granite game was settled with the arrival of the Brier. The change from a local pastime to a provincial and national event came with the Brier. The move to showcase the Canadian Championship by hosting it in every provincial capital and in major cities across the land, came from the Brier. The popularization of the sport, based on illustrious names and powerful corporate support, came from the Brier. The fact that all subsequent curling championships, both national and international, used the Brier as their model of excellence attests to its unique nature and stature.

Although there were a few famous names and teams prior to the Brier (the Toronto Red Jackets, and Winnipeg's Bob Dunbar team come to mind), from 1927 on the biggest names in curling have come from the Brier. The list is long and illustrious: Gordon Hudson, Howard (Pappy) Wood, Ken Watson, Don Duguid, Al (the Iceman) Hackner, Ed (Fast Eddy) Lukowich, Ed (the Wrench) Werenich, Kerry Burtnyk, Russ Howard, Kevin Martin, Jeff Stoughton, Randy Ferbey all became rightly famous, thanks to the Brier. And there are hundreds more. To earn a purple heart, the emblem of the provincial championship leading to play in the Brier, is the sine qua non of the sport in Canada; nothing else comes close.

Very few, if any, curlers wear their purple heart in club combat. It is considered a bit much to display the heart too ostentatiously. Perhaps it is framed in the rec room, or is left on the competition jacket, ready to be accompanied by a second purple heart, if the player should be so fortunate.

The story is told of one local club game at which a young curler, a legend in his own mind, shook hands with his elderly, white-haired opponent before the game, thinking with the bravado of youth that the ends ahead would be "a piece of cake." However, when the handshakes at the end of the game were completed, the youthful hotshot had been humiliated in quick time. As the curlers retired to the lounge, the standard question was asked: "What will you have to drink?"

"A coffee," said the patrician winner. As they chatted amiably, the hotshot allowed as how he always seemed to be up to his ankles in alligators when it

**It was in 1930 that one of the great names of Canadian curling—Howard Wood—won his first Brier title. He would win another in 1940. From l-r, Wood, Jimmy Congalton, Vic Wood, Lionel Wood.**

*Photo courtesy Western Pictorial Index A0103-03193.*

came time to deliver his final stones of the end, and said to the winner, "You played well tonight."

"Not really," was the reply. "Since I retired I've not curled as much as I'd like to."

"What did you do before you retired?" asked the kid, as he sneaked a look at the elder's name tag. Bill Beecroft, it said.

"I was a United Church minister in the North," he replied.

"That's an interesting badge," said the neophyte, pointing to the old-timer's cap. "I don't think I've ever seen that one before."

"No," came the reply, "there aren't too many of those around. (pause) I got that from Ken Watson the year we beat him in the Brier." Whap.

You could look it up in the Brier records. In 1936, Northern Ontario handed Manitoba its only loss that year, 10-6. The Rev. William Beecroft played second for Emmet Smith. Beecroft would gain two more purple hearts, in 1937 and 1939.

On a couple of occasions, the sponsor tried to change the purple heart to something else. In 1975, a new marketing executive with the Macdonald Company experimented with a different logo, figuring to switch if it caught on. He was soon made to understand that he had erred, and that particular experiment was quickly jettisoned. Then, in 1980, when the Labatt Brewing Company took over direction of the Brier, their marketing gurus decreed that the purple heart should be retired, to be replaced by an oval crest and pin, featuring the design of the newly crafted Labatt Tankard trophy. The howls of anguish from curlers across the country (led by Bob Weeks, editor of the *Ontario Curling Report*) quickly forced them to rethink the idea, and the purple heart was speedily reinstated.

Where did the purple heart come from? Quite simply, it was another trademark of the Macdonald Tobacco Company—a trademark that became more famous in curling than in its commercial life. In the early Macdonald days, those smokers who carved off pieces of tobacco from a plug of the product found a small tin heart pressed into the centre of the plug, along with the slogan "the heart of the tobacco." The same heart appeared on tins of pipe tobacco. Later, when other national championships were developed, each took the heart (same shape, different colour) as its identifying symbol.

A further measure of the impact of the first Brier came in 2000, when the original Macdonald Brier trophy, by now the property of the CCA, was refurbished, and the names of twenty years of Labatt Brier winners added to the names of the 1927–1979 champions. The elegant trophy remains one of Canada's proudest sporting emblems.

Unlike many other sporting championships, in which the players are hived off in glossy, luxurious surroundings, far from the fans who support the event, the Brier puts curlers and fans together, usually in a gathering place known as the Brier Patch. There had always been a meeting place at the Brier, but never one as elaborate as "the Patch." The first Brier Patch (under that name) was established by Don Pottinger's Brandon committee, in 1982. It has been a feature of the Brier ever since.

As the Brier moved into the new millennium, there were new forces at work. There had always been major bonspiels across the country that offered large prizes. In 1947, Nipawin (Saskatchewan) put up four brand new Hudson automobiles as prizes, and ushered in an era of carspiels. Howard (Pappy) Wood won that first carspiel in dramatic fashion. After he had thrown his final stone of the game, the crowd surged onto the ice to see the outcome, and blocked Wood's view of the shot. That didn't faze Pappy. He moved quickly across the ice to where the Hudson was being displayed, calmly opened the door and climbed in behind the wheel. In 1992, some of the elite players organized themselves into the World Curling Players' Association (WCPA) and a World Curling Tour (WCT) of major cashspiels was established, followed by a championship of top teams from the Tour.

The curling year was now neatly split in two. Cash bonspiels were held, in the main, before Christmas ("The Gold Trail," the CCN called it); from January on, provincial playdowns and national championships took over ("The Glory Trail").

In the 1990s, the CCA began to concentrate the Brier into larger arenas in major cities, particularly in the west. The move was not universally approved, particularly by curling hotbeds in eastern Canada, but it was the CCA share of profits, generated by the huge crowds at these Briers that was used to fund the CCA's ever-growing, grassroots programs. At the same time, many of the competing teams chafed at the restrictions placed on them at the Brier. Some players wanted cash prizes; others wanted to be able to wear the crests of firms that supported them throughout the year. When the national body ignored their concerns, the players became increasingly militant.

In 2001, the WCPA announced that it would organize its own major events, four in all, to be called the Grand Slam of Curling. Supported by the International Management Group (IMG), three GS events were scheduled (each with full television coverage), followed by the Players' Championship. What caused concern among curlers and fans alike was the stipulation that players who signed a contract to play in the Grand Slam also agreed to stay out of provincial championships leading to the Brier. This was quickly interpreted as a boycott of the Brier, and it split the ranks of curlers from coast to coast. Eighteen of the country's top teams enthusiastically endorsed the Slam, and signed the contract.

When the giant Finnish telecommunications firm, Nokia, assumed sponsorship of the Brier, the CCA was able to bring back the original Macdonald Brier tankard, refurbish it, and add the names of every Canadian champion since the event's inception.

*Photo courtesy Canadian Curling Association.*

Others refused. A threat to ostracize some of the teams who had refused to sign, and prohibit them from playing in WCT cashspiels, was quickly rescinded when the threat drew almost-universal condemnation. A few who did sign the contract subsequently broke ranks, saying they were unwilling to sacrifice the lure and lore of the Brier, its history and tradition. When they were suspended from Grand Slam play, for two years, their reaction ranged from ennui to enmity.

All signs at the time pointed to a gathering confrontation between the CCA and the WCPA, and between each group's rival marketing firms lurking in the background, IMG and the St. Clair Group.

Midway through the week of the 2002 Nokia Brier, there was a meeting involving representatives from the CCA management, the WCPA, and IMG. The objective appeared to be a search for a solution that would allow dissident WCPA curlers to continue with the Grand Slam and also play in their respective regions in an attempt to qualify for the Brier. Although progress appears slow, it is, nonetheless, progress.

# Ladeez and Gennulmen

**A word about language and usage to begin. As a journalist and a broadcaster,** I learned early how different the spoken word and the written word can be. For example, at each year's Air Canada Silver Broom, as the emcee at the opening gala, I would seek the audience's attention with the stentorian "Ladies and Gentlemen, Mesdames et Messieurs, Meine Damen und Herren." If I could have managed a few other languages, I would have used their words as well. "Men and women" just didn't work.

In the early days of curling, you were OK with 'ladies and gentlemen' in either the written, or the spoken, word. Not today. While it was relatively easy to shorten 'gentlemen' to 'men', it took somewhat longer to switch from 'ladies' to 'women'.

Indeed, there was much controversy involved. The Canadian Ladies' Curling Association never could agree to move to the more politically correct Canadian Women's Curling Association. Fortunately amalgamation with the Canadian Curling Association solved that problem. Still, years ago, it was tricky (as a male) to talk, or write, about 'ladies' curling'. Today there's no argument: it's 'women's curling'. Period. End of discussion. But no matter what term you use, the story of women's curling is a fascinating one.

When Canada was a young and growing country, where women worked as equals alongside their men, it's understandable they would want to curl as well. Early photos of women on outdoor ice show stones and brooms of course, and a variety of clothing styles: long skirts, coats, sweaters... and hats, always hats.

When the game moved indoors, many clubs relegated women to inconvenient times or separate areas. It would take many years for women to achieve equality within clubs, but by the end of the twentieth century, it was as common for women to become club presidents and managers, as it was for men.

In 1913, when a Ladies' event was added to the Manitoba Bonspiel, it must have encouraged women curlers everywhere. The same year, in Ontario, the OCA began a Ladies' Tankard event. Others followed suit.

It wasn't until the 1950s that women's curling moved beyond provincial borders in an organized way. At the time, there was a Western Canada Women's Championship, sponsored by the T. Eaton Company. In the east, there were individual provincial championships (Macdonald Tobacco, for example, sponsored a Quebec women's event) but no all-eastern championship. There was talk in women's curling circles about how wonderful it would be if they could have a championship of their own to emulate the Brier.

At the 1959 Western Canada Championship in Brandon, two eastern curlers, Hazel Watt of Thunder Bay and Rita Proulx of Quebec City, arrived to discuss a possible national event. Watt said she had a sponsor, but could not reveal its identity. Proulx indicated that Macdonald Tobacco was willing to extend its Quebec sponsorship into Ontario as a prelude to a wider event. But the Westerners were quite happy with the Eaton sponsorship, and they felt in no hurry to discuss a national championship. Discussions about the formation of a national women's body were put on hold.

By the fall of 1959, matters had changed. The West learned that Eaton's was not prepared to sponsor a national event, so when East and West met in Toronto, they were more amenable to listen to the earlier sponsorship proposals of Watt and Proulx. Some months later, in February of 1960, the Canadian Ladies' Curling Association was formed, with Hazel Watt as its first president. At the inaugural meeting, John Hull of Public Relations Services Limited (PRSL) was there to present a sponsorship plan on behalf of Dominion Stores Limited. It was one of the few times in curling history (up to then) that a sponsor, intent on targeting a specific demographic—women—approached the sport, and not vice versa. For women's curling, it was a "first" of considerable magnitude.

**The ladies at Indian Head, Saskatchewan, made a fashion statement with this photo c. 1905.**

*Courtesy Western Canada Pictorial Index, #A0231-07429.*

From there, matters moved quickly. Eaton's Western Canadian champions, the Joyce McKee team from Saskatoon, which included Sylvia Fedoruk, Donna Belding, and Muriel Coben, was flown to Oshawa to play the winner of a hastily assembled Eastern Canadian championship. Ruth Smith of Lacolle, Quebec, came out of a five-team playdown, but lost the initial Dominion Diamond D championship to Saskatchewan's McKee.

The following year saw the Diamond D turn to the Brier format of ten provincial teams seeking a national crown. The teams were assembled in Ottawa, and the event proved instantly popular. The 1961 title was won (as in

1960) by the Joyce McKee team, this time with a new front end of Barbara
MacNevin and Rosa McFee to accompany Sylvia Fedoruk at third. McKee would
go on to win a third crown, as skip, in 1969, and three more Canadian championships as second for Vera Pezer. Between them, McKee and Pezer helped establish and solidify the stature of the Canadian Women's Championship.

It wasn't only male champion curlers who went on to become Lieutenant-
Governor in their province, as had Errick Willis (1932 Olympic winner) in
Manitoba. Sylvia Fedoruk would cap a marvellous multi-faceted academic,

**In 1960, these five skips played off to determine an Eastern Canada team to meet Joyce McKee's Western Canadian champions. From l-r are: Mono Comeau (NB), Pauline Burden (PEI), Elsie Forsyth (ON), Marge Harris (NS) and Ruth Smith (QC). The Eastern title was won by Smith.**
*Photo courtesy of Sylvia Fedoruk.*

research, and sporting career when she was named the Queen's representative in Saskatchewan, as Lieutenant-Governor of that curling-obsessed province. Years later, she would recall her first brush with a royal representative. It was in 1961.

Said Fedoruk, "The participants in the Diamond D that year were rushed off the ice between draws to have an opportunity to be introduced to Governor General Georges Vanier and Mrs. Vanier at Rideau Hall. We had no chance to change.

"During our hurried ride from the Ottawa Hunt Club to Government House, our driver gave us a crash course in protocol. After reaching under her seat for her tam (and dusting it off), she said that we as curlers were exempt from wearing hats, but were expected to wear gloves and to curtsy.

"You have the photograph before you [p. 131]. We're in our bulky curling sweaters trying to curtsy before their excellencies. I was very embarrassed having to shake Madame Vanier's hand using a very grubby curling glove. Somehow, Barbara MacNevin, who was directly behind me, managed to find or borrow a pair of clean white cotton gloves."

Other champion women curlers also became prominent at the political level. The 1963 championship skip, Mabel DeWare of New Brunswick, went on to become president of the CLCA, a provincial cabinet minister, and eventually a member of the Canadian Senate.

After five years of Dominion Diamond D play, there were rumblings of discontent within the fledgling administration of women's curling. The sponsor, Dominion Stores, left all matters to the CLCA and PRSL. There were some who felt that Watt, as CLCA president, and supposedly neutral, was much too closely allied to PRSL (and Dominion Stores) and indeed, the words "Hull's puppet" were occasionally heard. In those early years, a variety of problems were brought to the CLCA's annual meetings until, in 1967, there was a "High Noon at the OK Corral" showdown.

On the evening before the 1967 annual meeting, John Hull presented a paper to the executive of the CLCA entitled "Sponsor's Policy." It was a difficult document for the women to accept, and Hull was invited by president Addie Roy to present it to the full meeting of representatives the following day. According to those present at the meeting, it was an acrimonious occasion, capped by a "take it or leave it" ultimatum from Hull: accept the policy by six o'clock or

**The 1961 Dominion Diamond D
champions from Saskatchewan pose
with the first trophy for Canadian
Women's curling supremacy. From l-r
are Sylvia Fedoruk, Hazel Watt (president
CLCA), Joyce McKee, Scott Feggans
(Dominion Stores Ltd.), Barbara
MacNevin, and Rosa McFee.**
*Photo courtesy of Sylvia Fedoruk.*

Dominion Stores is no longer sponsor of your championship. Following some afternoon discussions with a lawyer, the women decided to leave it.

This created another dubious first in Canadian curling: a sponsor "invited" to depart the scene. One unfortunate side effect of this was the destruction of all written material pertaining to the early history of the event.

The CLCA operated the championship on its own from 1968–71. When Sylvia Fedoruk (who had played third for Joyce McKee twelve years earlier) assumed the presidency of the CLCA in 1971, one of her priorities was to find a sponsor for the "orphan" event. As in most of her endeavours, Fedoruk was successful and, in 1972, on behalf of the CLCA, she signed a contract that saw

Years after she had served a couple of terms as Lieutenant-Governor of Saskatchewan, the Hon. Sylvia Fedoruk would recall, with wry humour, the occasion during the 1961 championship when the Joyce McKee team was rushed from the rink to meet Governor General Georges Vanier and Madame Vanier at Rideau Hall. Not having her white gloves handy, Fedoruk had to make do with her curling gloves!

*Photo courtesy of Sylvia Fedoruk.*

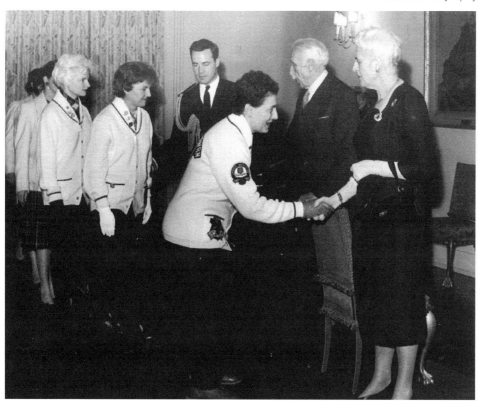

the Macdonald Tobacco Company assume sponsorship of the championship, and in an obvious move, rename the event The Lassie, after the company's trademark Scots lady.

More importantly, the Macdonald Tobacco style of sponsorship had arrived. David Stewart and his coonskin coat had come to the world of women's curling. The company would put up the necessary dollars to make the event a success, and would provide the promotional and public relations support to ensure a championship event with flair. The CLCA would look after the essentials related

to competition and the development of women's curling. It was a happy time for the women.

The first Lassie championship, in 1972, was won by Vera Pezer of Saskatchewan, a repeat of her victory from the previous year. When Pezer won again in 1973, it gave her and teammates Sheila Rowan, Joyce McKee, and Lenore Morrison three consecutive championships—a remarkable record, unmatched in the annals of either the Brier or Hearts/Lassie/Diamond D play. (There would, however, be three-time consecutive winners, in later years, in both Senior Men's and Senior Women's play.)

The happy Lassie arrangement lasted till 1979 when Macdonald Tobacco, under increasingly heavy pressure from the Canadian government's anti-tobacco thrust, reluctantly withdrew its support of both the Brier and the Lassie.

**David M. Stewart helped provide a send-off for the 1979 Lassie champions to the first World Women's Championship in Scotland, when he put his trademark coonskin coat on skip Lindsay Sparkes' shoulders. The other members of the '79 Canadian championship team are (l-r) Lorraine Bowles, Robin Wilson and Dawn Knowles.**

*Photo courtesy the Macdonald Stewart Foundation.*

Once again, the women were on their own, and for the next two years, the CLCA operated its own championship.

It was in the last year of Macdonald sponsorship that the curling women of the world united to form their own global championship, with the first Ladies' World Curling Championship (LWCC) title shoot taking place in Perth, Scotland. The event went through some name changes: World Ladies' Curling Championship (WLCC) and eventually, World Women's Curling Championship (WWCC). The Canadian team in 1979, the winner of the last Lassie, was a B.C. foursome skipped by Lindsay Sparkes, with Dawn Knowles at third, Robin

"Bob Stewart always had an active hand in the menu selection for the Victory Banquet. For years he had suggested beets, but I managed to ignore this (I hate beets). In 1988 (by now he was president of Scott Paper) he insisted. However, we had a major challenge in moving 500 guests up a narrow staircase from the reception area to the ballroom. As a result, all the vegetables (including the beets) were burned and had to be replaced. I'll never forget Bob's remarks that night when he said, 'I have been trying for years to get Robin to put beets on the menu. I have accomplished that. I still have to find a way to get her to put them on your plates.' Ten years later, when he went in for surgery, I sent a beets bouquet to his hospital room."

—Robin Wilson, Scott Tournament of Hearts Co-ordinator

Wilson at second, and lead Lorraine Bowles. Unhappily for the Canadians, they lost that first world event to a Swiss team skipped by Gaby Casanova.

In a manner similar to Sylvia Fedoruk's involvement with the national championship and Macdonald Tobacco, the B.C. second, Robin Wilson, soon became involved with a new sponsor of women's curling, Scott Paper.

In 1979, at the time Macdonald Tobacco announced its imminent departure from Canadian curling, Wilson was leaving the employ of Scott Paper to have a child. In 1980, she was invited by John Leonard of the Walker Leonard Advertising Agency to help prepare a proposal inviting Scott Paper to become sponsor of the Canadian Women's Championship. The proposal was accepted by Scott, and in 1981, by the CLCA. In February of 1982, the first Scott Tournament of Hearts was held in Regina, with Wilson acting as co-ordinator. When the ad agency was sold in 1987, Wilson formed her own company, Robin Wilson and Associates, to handle the administration and promotion of the Tournament of Hearts. She quickly became the dominant figure in the newly minted Scott event. Her stature as a former champion herself, together with her promotional background, ensured the success of the event. Today, the Scott Tournament of Hearts is Canada's longest-running, sponsored, national event, and Wilson has become the dean of championship curling administrators.

The winner of the first Tournament of Hearts, in 1982, was Colleen Jones of Nova Scotia, ably supported by her two sisters, Monica Jones and Barbara Jones-Gordon, and Kay Smith. Colleen Jones would go on to skip three more Canadian winners, in 1999, 2001, and 2002, making her the first women's skip to win four national crowns. She had less luck internationally, winning only one world title, in 2001, in that 20-year span.

Even when she was being fêted for her record-setting fourth title, Colleen Jones graciously suggested that she did not consider herself in the same category as Sandra Schmirler of Regina. Starting in 1993, Schmirler, then Sandra Peterson, put together an enviable record, along with teammates Jan Betker, Joan McCusker, and Marcia Gudereit. The Schmirler foursome won back-to-back Scott Tournament of Hearts titles. Three years later, in 1997, the team captured their third national title, and then qualified to represent Canada at the 1998 Winter Olympics, when curling became an official medal sport. After winning an Olympic gold medal in Karuizawa, Japan, they returned to Regina as Team Canada in the 1998 Scott championship, with only a few days' rest. Jet lag finally caught up with them toward the end of the competition, and they ran out of gas in their bid for a fourth Scott title. Tragedy struck in 2000, when the 36-year-old Schmirler succumbed to cancer, shortly after the birth of her second daughter. Her story, and the story of the Schmirler team, has been told in two eloquent books: *Gold on Ice: the Story of the Sandra Schmirler Curling Team* by Guy Scholz, and *Sandra Schmirler, The Queen of Curling* by Perry Lefko.

**The Scott Tournament of Hearts trophy: respected, sought-after, cherished.**

*Photo courtesy Scott Paper and Scott Tournament of Hearts.*

The combination of adroit promotion, skilled play, and full television coverage helped the Scott Tournament of Hearts to become a vital component of the Canadian curling scene. It also helped that one of the assets of the TV coverage was the outstanding analysis provided by the 1985 Scott champion and gold medallist at the 1988 Calgary Winter Games, Linda Moore. As with the Brier, until a team made its reputation at the Scott Tournament of Hearts (or either of its predecessors, the Diamond D and The Lassie), it was not considered a household name. Some of those household names that stand out include foursomes with such outstanding skips as Joyce McKee, Vera Pezer, Lindsay Sparkes, Linda Moore, Heather Houston, Connie Laliberte, Marilyn (Darte) Bodogh, Colleen Jones, and, of course, Sandra Schmirler.

# CHAPTER 11

# Offspring of the Brier

**The success and enthusiasm generated by the Brier led to a full family of similar** competitions which followed, in most cases, a similar pattern of regional/provincial championships leading to a national event. The official ones are easy to list: school (later changed to junior) championships, for young men and women; the national mixed; and senior events, for older men and women.

In addition, there is a veritable army of "unofficial" championships, some accepted as long-time events, some as curio events. We have already seen how involved the military, and by extension, the police, have been in the history of Canadian curling. So it is no surprise that there is a national police championship, and a national firefighters' championship. And a national championship involving the Canadian Legion. There are others.

Some years ago, a left-hander named John Bryant started a "World Left-Handers" Championship at the Oakville CC in Ontario, an event that now includes women as well. For a few short years, there was a trencherman's bonspiel (sponsored by Shopsy Foods) known as the World Heavyweight Curling Championship. In that one, teams were ineligible unless the four players together could hit 1,000 pounds [450 kg] on the scales, and each member of the team had to weigh in at a minimum of 225 pounds [101 kg]. The banquet (of Shopsy

**In 2002, the WCF sanctioned a World Wheelchair Curling Championship, and the competition in Sursee, Switzerland, saw Canada win the silver medal, thanks to the team skipped by Chris Dawe.**
*Photo courtesy Canadian Curling Association.*

Foods, naturally) was a classic of its genre. The 'spiel attracted a roster of prodigious players, including such smaller big men as world champion Chuck Hay (Scotland) and Brier champ Hector Gervais (Canada). There were a number of Canadian Football League players, a smattering of burly policemen and one company CEO who made the 225-pound mark, but was lean, since his weight was spread over 6' 8" of height.

Every service club worth its salt has either a local, provincial, regional, or national title-shoot. The Rotary Club even has an international bonspiel, Scotland vs Canada. In 2002, with the sanction of the WCF, Sursee (in Switzerland) hosted the first-ever World Wheelchair Curling Championship, where

**Chris Dawe in action at the first World Wheelchair Curling Championship in 2002.**
*Photo courtesy Canadian Curling Association.*

Canada won a silver medal. The same year saw the Ford World Championships in Bismarck, North Dakota, play host to the first officially sanctioned World Seniors Championship. There's a national championship for blind and visually impaired people. And one for the deaf.

There is a plethora of career-related curling events—from doctors to lawyers to teachers and preachers, and, it is assumed, candlestick makers. During the years of the Air Canada Silver Broom, 1968–1985, there was an annual media event called the Brass Whisk that was more of a one-off fun day than anything else. But it is recorded that, early on, one media curler took the Brass Whisk so seriously that he altered his personal letterhead to indicate he was "world media curling champion," a somewhat arrogant claim that, once discovered by his fellow media mavens, had him blushing in embarrassment and rushing to get rid of the offending stationery.

Another Silver Broom event, the Grand Transatlantic Match, was begun in Karlstad in 1977 and eventually, when Pacific curling nations entered the world event, was renamed the Grand Transoceanic Match, or GTM. Patterned after Scotland's Grand Match (North of Scotland versus South), the GTM allowed spectators from one side of the world to challenge those from the other side in a total points event. The dividing line was established differently each year. There was even one year, in Garmisch-Partenkirchen, when the games began each night at midnight, in honour of the eccentric King Ludwig of Bavaria, who would only travel at night.

Most of these matches were clashes in the time-honoured custom of early Canadian curling, when even the flimsiest excuse was sufficient to arrange a game of fun and sociability.

The Canadian events that are officially sanctioned by the CCA (in addition to the men's and women's championships) are the Junior, Senior, and the Mixed events. Perhaps a word about each would help indicate the strength of history each one contains.

### School Curling, or Junior Curling

In 1950, championed by legendary Brier hero Ken Watson, a national School Championship for boys was instituted, with the opening event being held in Quebec City. Pepsi Cola of Canada was the sponsor. There had been regional and provincial school championships in western Canada before then, first sponsored by the *Winnipeg Free Press* newspaper, but it wasn't until 1950 that school curling made it to the national stage.

School curling was said to be the only high school sport that provided its devotees with a national championship. Not all school boards were in favour, for the event removed forty to fifty teens from school for a week of play each February. Nevertheless, school curling became the next national event after the Brier, predating national competition at the ladies' level, or mixed curling, or seniors'. Many of the early organizers, nationally, were school teachers or board of education administrators who felt that the week away from classes in a different part of the country was a valuable education in itself.

Nor should school curling be overlooked as a major catalyst in the expansion of the game from coast to coast to coast. The sport leaped ahead as teams were organized in high schools large and small, in cities and towns across the country. The costs involved were minimal. Equipment was inexpensive, local clubs were usually willing to provide ice at a low cost, or no cost. A large contingent of players was not necessary. Nor were size and strength important factors. Four friends could join forces and shoot for the brass ring. Supervision

was relatively easy, and curling's dedication to proper etiquette and behaviour helped the sport to grow, both athletically and administratively. "The curling heroes of tomorrow," it was said, "were created in the classrooms of today." Those heroes came together annually, in a carbon copy of the Brier.

Saskatchewan's Bill Clarke, with Gary Carlson, Ian Innes, and Harold Grassie, won that first School Championship of 1950, and while he went on to become an all-star football player with the Saskatchewan Roughriders, Clarke was never able to make it to the Brier. Another Saskatchewan curler, name of Ernie Richardson, always seemed to be in his way.

**Three eyes are better than one would seem to be in the indication in this 1979 game. Bill Carey (left) and skip Barry Fry eyeball a tricky situation.**

*Photo by Michael Burns.*

Winning the Canadian School title became almost a curse when it came to winning the Brier. It wasn't until 1978, twenty-eight years after the start of the Schools competition, that a schoolboy winner was able to win the Brier. Ed Lukowich, then from Saskatchewan, who played third for his brother Mike in 1962, became the first Schoolboy winner to tame the Brier. "Cool Hand Luke" would go on to win a second Brier in 1986. While many outstanding younger players have gone on to play in the Brier, the number who have been able to win two Canadian titles—a School and a Brier—can be counted on the fingers of both hands. In fact, you would only need seven fingers—six for Alberta curlers and one for a Manitoban! Alphabetically, the seven shooters are John Ferguson, Neil Houston, Ed Lukowich, Kevin Martin, Jonathan Mead, Dan Petryk and Scott Pfeiffer.

The school champions also helped change the rules of the game. Remember Stan Austman and his slide the length of the ice in 1954 (from chapter 8)? That was not the only occasion when school-age curlers prompted a revision of the rules. In 1958, when a school-age Winnipeg team put a last-minute entry into the Manitoba Bonspiel, they were able to qualify for the provincial playdowns as one of 64 teams vying for the coveted purple heart. To the surprise of most observers, this School team of Terry Braunstein, Ron Braunstein, Ray Turnbull, and Jack Van Hellemond won the Manitoba title, and then set off for the Victoria Brier. When they arrived they found they could wear their Manitoba purple heart where ice and competition was involved, but being under age according to Canada's liquor laws, they could not join their fellow competitors where ice and alcohol were involved! That too prompted a rule change regarding the eligibility of teams for School play and for the Brier. The total age of the four young sharpshooters, incidentally, equalled the age of Andy Grant, the Ontario skip that year!

Some twenty or so years later, in what many considered a dubious decision, the annual School Championship was changed to a Junior Championship. Why dubious? Two reasons. A positive reason involved the international move at the time to establish a World Junior Championship, in which the age limit would be 21 years. Other than in Scotland, school curling did not exist anywhere outside of Canada, so a world school competition wasn't worth considering. There was, however, junior curling in enough countries to warrant a world junior event, so junior curling it was. While some felt that a team of Canadian school champions, maximum age 18 or 19, might be at a disadvantage when playing another country's 21-year-olds, there were others who felt that Canada's strength in numbers more than made up for the age difference. In any event, when Canada joined the junior crowd, it was easy to move to a 21-year age limit.

The down-side of the decision saw the event move out of the schools and into the curling clubs, where, said observers, the competition would limit the event to sons of club members. School competition had no such restriction. Indeed, many of the country's top curlers came into the game from school curling, where club membership was not essential. Years later, many agreed that the loss of curling in the schools had been unfortunate, to say the least. Others, not so sanguine, called it a disaster.

The final piece to be inserted into the mosaic that forms the Canadian Championship scene was the junior women's event. Here too, there is a smidgen of controversy about its formative years. Did it begin in 1971? Or in 1972? The 1971 championship was held in Vancouver and while Canadian

Curling Association records show it as an official event (Calgary's Shelby McKenzie, Marlene Pargeter, Arleen Hrdlicka, and Debbie Goliss were the winners), other accounts report it as an unofficial championship, since only four western provinces competed. In 1972, when the event was held in Winnipeg, the number of competing provincial teams had doubled to eight, with only Saskatchewan and New Brunswick missing. That year was a hometown delight as Manitoba's Pidzarko twins (Chris and Cathy, with Beth Brunsden and Barbara Rudolph) won the title, undefeated.

By 1973, all ten provinces were represented, with later entries (as in the other national events) added from the territories. Today a total of 13 provincial/territorial champions meet annually. The very nature of junior curling, with its age limit, means that few winners are able to repeat their first triumph. Even so, five teams have been able to win a pair of titles over the past thirty and more years. The Pidzarkos repeated as national champions in 1974, as did Alberta's Cathy King in 1977 and '78. In 1975, Colleen Rudd played third on the winning Saskatchewan team and then skipped her province to another title in 1976. Another pair of twins, Jodie and Julie Sutton of B.C., were winners in 1986, and in 1987, when Jodie was travelling abroad, Julie took over as skip and won again. In 2001 and 2002, Suzanne Gaudet of P.E.I. became the most recent repeat winner.

Canada's title teams in domestic play have also been hugely successful internationally. In the period between 1988 (when the world junior women's championships began) and 2002, Canada won 7 of 15 of the global titles. Scotland won four crowns, Sweden won twice, Switzerland and the USA once each.

## World Junior Curling Championships

The junior men's world event grew out of a venture started in Toronto by a clutch of enthusiastic curlers at the East York Curling Club in the early 1970s. When one of Canada's major companies, Uniroyal of Canada, was approached to provide funding for the East York Masters (as it was then called), they were more than willing to assist, but Bob Sutherland, the Uniroyal Director of Public

Relations, insisted the competition should become a formal world championship. This meant a request to the International Curling Federation to recognize it as such. Some member countries (notably Scotland) were concerned that a World Junior Championship might detract from the successor to the Scotch Cup, the Air Canada Silver Broom, which had begun in 1968. When they were satisfied (by Air Canada and most other countries) that a World Junior Championship was a good idea, the Uniroyal World Junior (Men's) Championship was born. The year was 1975. In the ensuing period 1975—2002, Canada's Junior Men have brought home a total of twelve world titles, while the next nearest successful country, Scotland, has eight. Other world winners among the Junior men are Sweden and Switzerland (three apiece) and the USA (two). The only two-time World winners hail from Canada, in the persons of skips Paul Gowsell (and his lead Kelly Stearne) in 1976 and '78, and John Morris (skip) Craig Savill (third) and lead Brent Laing in 1998 and 1999.

As mentioned earlier, among the world junior women (who began their international play in 1988), Canada has captured seven global crowns. Only Scotland has been able to celebrate repeat junior winners. In 1990, Kirsty Addison skipped her team to victory, and three years later, as Kirsty Hay, she won a second world title. Gillian Barr was with her on both occasions, and indeed Barr had skipped Scotland to victory in the interim (1992), making her the only three-time World Junior winner in history.

## The Canadian Mixed Championship

In the heady days following World War II, and with the possibilities of being able to add artificial ice, club curling expanded exponentially. Nowhere was this more evident than in Toronto, where the "original" four clubs of the city soon exploded into 24, 25, and 26 separate operations. Nor did that include clubs that were just outside the city boundaries.

One aspect of this expansion was the addition of mixed curling—two men and two women to a team—and the growth of a city-wide mixed championship.

The O'Keefe Brewing Company was the initial sponsor of the Toronto Mixed Bonspiel in the mid-fifties. And within a year or two of its start-up success, the brewery dreamed of expanding the event to a national championship. Still, there was hesitation among the promoters of the idea. In the society of the mid-twentieth century, their concerns now seem dated, but forty and more years ago, the sponsor was faced with a nagging worry. Brewery executives were concerned about how they would be perceived if teams, composed of other than married couples, were to participate in an event where all would be housed in a hotel away from home, for over a week's time. When it was pointed out that any couple desirous of a quiet (and illicit) weekend would hardly go to the trouble of winning a provincial title and then spending a week at a national championship for their tryst, the sponsor's worries were laid to rest. The first O'Keefe Canadian Mixed championship was held in Toronto in 1964. Under the guidance of incoming CCA president Frank Sargent of Thunder Bay, the event proved successful and quickly became a staple of the Canadian championship curling scene. Ernie Boushy of Manitoba (with Ina Light, Garry DeBlonde, and Bea McKenzie) won the opening crown, and with Betty Hird replacing McKenzie two years later, Boushy won again in 1966. In the same fashion as the Brier and the Tournament of Hearts, the Mixed attracted many of the country's best curlers. To name just a few, there were Larry McGrath, Rick Folk, Barry Fry, Rick Lang, Steve Ogden, Jeff Stoughton, and Randy Woytowich among the male players; Colleen Jones, Marnie McNiven, Dorenda Schoenhals, Pat Sanders, Karen Fallis, Dawn Ventura, and Kathy Fahlman among the women.

### Seniors Curling

In 1965, Leo Johnson of Manitoba, the 1934 Brier champion, became the first winner of the Seagram Stone, the newly-minted Canadian Senior Men's title. Along with Marno Fredericksen, Fred Smith and Cliff Wise, Johnson's victory helped solidify the concept of Seniors curling. It wasn't until 1973 that a Senior Women's championship was added to the roster of Canadian events, and that year it was

a British Columbia team, led by Ada Calles, with Ina Hansen, May Shaw, and Barbara Weir, who helped inaugurate the Senior Women's competition. In 2000, Glasgow, Scotland, added a Seniors exhibition series to its hosting of the World Championships, and in 2002, the World Seniors Championships became an official part of the Worlds in Bismarck, North Dakota. Canada's Senior Women's Champions, skipped by Anne Dunn, won the inaugural event: the USA men (Larry Johnston) took the men's title.

All of these outstanding competitions were valid offspring of the Brier. All adopted the same format. All provided yearly—and worthy—champions. All are a part of Canada's curling history.

More recently, the CCA, and the WCF, have added a pair of national and international events to the curling calendar: The Canada Cup of Curling and the Continental Cup. The inaugural Continental Cup (the international event), held in Regina in November of 2002, pitted six World teams (selected by the WCF) against six North American teams (selected by the CCA and USCA). In addition to regular curling, the Continental Cup featured a Points (Hot Shot) competition, Mixed Doubles matches and a Skins event, all for a prize purse of $200,000 ($120,000 to the winners; $80,000 to the losers).

The thing that sets the Canada Cup apart from the CCA's other national events is the fact there is a prize pot of $240,000 up for grabs. Kamloops, B.C., agreed to host the Canada Cup in its formative years, starting in January of 2003. Ten men's teams and ten women's teams from all parts of Canada are featured.

# CHAPTER 12

# The World Championships

**Sometime in the late 1950s, John Hull, and his firm, Public Relations Services** Limited, came up with the concept of a Canada versus Scotland championship. The idea went from PRSL to the McKim Advertising Agency, and from there to one of McKim's clients, the Scotch Whisky Association. They liked the idea, and agreed to sponsor it. It wasn't hard to find a suitable name: the Scotch Cup. However, when presented to officials of the Dominion Curling Association, they reacted with something approaching ennui. They feared it would detract from the Brier.

That did not deter Hull, who hired Stan Houston, a well-known Toronto sportswriter who went on to become one of the city's best public relations executives. Houston's job was to develop all elements of the event in co-operation with the sponsor. There was already one Canada-Scotland competition, the Strathcona Cup, which had been ongoing for some fifty-plus years, and which brought together curlers from both countries every five years or so. But it was as much a social as a competitive event, with the main requirement being the ability to reach into one's pocket and foot the considerable bill covering travel, hotel, meals, and the odd libation with new-found friends.

Perhaps it was an omen of bad luck, but Canada's Brier champs of 1965 posed with the Scotch Cup prior to the world series. It was the closest they came to holding the coveted cup. From l-r are Terry Braunstein, Don Duguid, Gord McTavish, and Ray Turnbull.

*Photo by Michael Burns.*

What Hull and Houston had in mind was something different—a meeting of champions. Into the mix came two key curlers and personalities: Jock Waugh of Scotland and Ken Watson of Canada. Waugh, a gregarious soul, was the grain buyer for the Distillers Company, at that time Scotland's largest distiller, and a key member of the Scotch Whisky Association. Watson, of course, was Canada's best-known and most famous curler.

It was agreed that Waugh would look after the Scottish end of arrangements, while Watson would take care of curling matters in Canada. Houston's mandate included the many administrative and promotional details. Neither the Royal

Caledonian Curling Club nor the DCA were involved in the deal, to their considerable chagrin. Later, each would swallow its pride and admit that the Scotch Cup was a grand idea, on a grand scale.

There were a number of early problems. In Canada, most clubs were owned by their curling members and catered to a large number of players. All the Brier required was that all team members should come from the same club, a stipulation that was easily handled. In Scotland, however, most ice rinks were (and are) private, commercial enterprises that rent ice to any number of curling clubs, as well as to skaters. The stipulation for the Scots championship was the same as

**Three of the hard-sweeping Richardsons at work: Wes, Sam, and Ernie Richardson work the brooms.**

*Photo by Michael Burns.*

the Brier—the four curlers must hail from the same club—but there was a major difference. Most of the Scottish clubs were small, ranging from twenty to thirty members, of all ages. Getting a title team from an ice rink, with its many clubs, would have been easy. But finding four top-level curlers who belonged to the same club proved a significant stumbling block. That matter would not be resolved until 1963, when the RCCC deemed it acceptable to field a Scottish team composed of any four Scots curlers.

Then there were the rule differences: the length of the slide in delivery; the kind of hack to be used; who could sweep where and when. These were but a few of the items to be discussed.

In 1960, when they arrived back in Regina carrying the Scotch Cup with them, the Richardsons, led by Ernie and followed by Arnold, Sam, and Wes, were welcomed with enthusiasm.

*Photo by Michael Burns.*

The first Scotch Cup series was slated for 1959, and shortly after the Brier had been completed in Quebec City, the new Canadian champions, a little-known family foursome from Regina, flew to Scotland for a five-game touring series against the Scots champions. It turned out to be a serendipitous occasion. The likeable and youthful Canadians—Ernie, Arnold, Garnet (Sam), and Wes Richardson—were drawn against a much older foursome skipped by Willie Young.

**Forty-some years after their four Scotch Cup wins (1959, 1960, 1962, 1963), the famed Richardsons of Regina were honoured at a sold-out, packed-house banquet in Regina. From l-r are Wes Richardson, Arnold Richardson, Ernie Richardson, and Sam Richardson.**

*Photo by Ardith Stephanson, courtesy Canadian Curling News.*

Little did either Watson or Waugh know that the Richardsons would represent Canada in four of the first five years of the Scotch Cup. But what representatives they were!

Years later, Chuck Hay, arguably one of Scotland's greatest curlers, summed up the early years of the Scotch Cup this way. "From Day One," he wrote (in a private letter), "the Scotch Cup was an outstanding success. It caught the imagination of the Scottish curlers. Its future was ensured. Canada dominated the play but the Scots enjoyed watching the young Canadians curl. It was the marvelous way Ernie and his team conducted themselves both on and off the ice that sealed the success of the Scotch Cup.

"They won their games easily but never belittled or humiliated their opposition. They had such charm, charisma and a wonderful sense of sportsmanship. In spite of the fact they won easily, the Scots could not get enough of the Richardson magic.

"It may seem 'corny' to heap all this praise on the Richardson team," concluded Hay, "but their part in establishing the Scotch Cup was so important and so well done, they deserve all the praise. It was because of them that we all sit back and enjoy today's World Curling Championships."

From a two-country event, Canada and Scotland, in 1959, the Scotch Cup grew to an eight-country competition by adding the USA in 1961, Sweden in 1962, Norway and Switzerland in 1964, France in 1966, and Germany in 1967.

Although nominally an invitational event, to most curlers the Scotch Cup was accorded the same status as a fully-sanctioned world championship. In its nine years of existence, Canada won seven of the titles (four by the Richardsons)

while the USA won in 1965 with their Hall of Famer, Bud Somerville, and Scotland took the other crown when Chuck Hay won the final Scotch Cup in 1967.

About the time that Somerville was winning the Cup, and giving it an air of legitimacy world-wide, some of the lesser members of the Scotch Whisky Association felt their sponsorship of the Scotch Cup had served its purpose. They were able to convince the majority of their fellow members that the Scotch Cup should be mothballed following the 1967 championship.

The logo of the International Curling Federation, forerunner of the World Curling Federation. In its move to gain favour with the International Olympic Committee, and to avoid confusion with the International Canoe Federation, the ICF changed its name and initials.

*Logo courtesy* Canadian Curling News.

With the imminent loss of such a growing world event, it fell to Canadian broadcaster and sports entrepreneur Doug Smith of Montreal to find a replacement. He asked for, and received, from the RCCC, a six-month option to find a Canadian sponsor. Smith soon found interest from Air Canada, but his option lapsed before he could finalize the details. Once the option had run out, Air Canada moved to deal directly with the RCCC, and quickly finalized its sponsorship of the world championship. The announcement of the new world event, and its new name—the Air Canada Silver Broom—was made in December of 1967, with the first Silver Broom slated for the following March in Pte. Claire, Quebec. Between December and March, agreement was obtained from all the competing nations and the fledgling International Curling Federation (at that time a committee of the RCCC), that the Silver Broom would be sanctioned as a true World Curling Championship.

When the first Silver Broom was held in 1968, three teams dominated: Bud Somerville of the USA, Chuck Hay of Scotland, and Calgary's Ron Northcott. In the round-robin series, Scotland went undefeated (7-0), while Canada (6-1) and the USA (5-2) placed second and third. After ousting Somerville in the semifinal, Northcott moved on to hand Hay his first loss of the week and claimed his second world title (the first had come in 1966). The classy Calgary curler would win again the following year, giving him three world crowns in four years of play. In each case, he had the same front end of Fred Storey and Bernie Sparkes, but enlisted a different third player each year. In 1966, it was George Fink; in 1968, Jimmy Shields. Dave Gerlach was the third in 1969.

The Silver Broom remained an eight-country competition until 1973, when Italy and Denmark were added, to increase the roster of competing teams to ten,

and the Worlds has remained at ten countries ever since. Over the years, a system of qualification was established that said the ten competing nations would consist of seven European nations, two North American countries and one from the Pacific region. And no matter where the World event was held, the host nation would be given an automatic entry.

Since 1968 and the first Scotch Cup, Canada has been the dominant country. Of 44 world events (for men), Canada has won 27 titles, while the others have been spread between the USA and Sweden (four each), Scotland, Switzerland and Norway (three apiece).

The early years of the Silver Broom were heady times. The level of competition was spotty at first, but the carrot of an all-expense-paid trip to participate in a bona fide world event was enough to attract the best curlers in

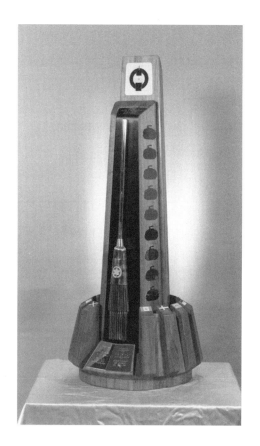

**This is the second Air Canada Silver Broom trophy, designed by Keith Jones and crafted in Toronto. The first Silver Broom was a quickly constructed trophy that had to be developed in a rush to meet initial sponsorship deadlines.**

*Photo courtesy* Canadian Curling News.

each of the participating countries. It was also enough to prompt a number of the countries to seek help in improving their competitive abilities. So as the years progressed, the teams—and the calibre of competition—improved.

So did the event itself. Spectator interest mushroomed. Host committees worked hard to make the event as attractive a visit for supporters as possible. The formation, in 1970, of a rollicking group known as the ACSBPHAICBJS —Air Canada Silver Broom Pond Hoppers And International Curling Buff Jet Set—created a camaraderie that was totally consistent with the sociability of curling, and helped create an atmosphere around the World Championship that was beguiling. And unique.

For the first five years of its existence, the Silver Broom was an enjoyable, but intimate, occasion. All that changed with the 1973 Broom in Regina. An enthusiastic committee, headed by Laurie Artiss, turned the event that year into "a happening," and suddenly the Silver Broom moved to a new plateau. Artiss, who would later become a Canadian representative to the ICF, was the driving force in changing the Worlds from a pleasant, albeit sleepy, event into a bustling, high-energy occasion. He also helped put Regina on the international curling map when he later chaired a successful Brier, in 1976, and a second Silver Broom, in 1983.

Over the course of the first 14 years of world play, Canada was the dominant country, winning 12 titles. Only Bud Somerville (USA) and Chuck Hay (Scotland) broke the Canadian skein of wins. The last Canadian win, before a seven-year drought struck, was in 1972, when Winnipeg's Orest Meleschuk won the Silver Broom in Garmisch-Partenkirchen, Germany. That drought was turned into a rather fanciful story all its own—"The Curse of LaBonte"—by an enthusiastic

It was a significant "first" in Regina, 1973, when Sweden's Kjell Oscarius team won the Air Canada Silver Broom—the first time a European team won a world curling title. From l-r are Boa Carlman (lead), Tom Schaeffer (second), Kjell Oscarius (skip), and Bengt Oscarius (third).

*Photo by Michael Burns.*

(and imaginative) writer in 1980 in Moncton. Full details are set out in the following chapter.

A second plateau of excellence was established in 1978 when Vic Palmer and a coterie of curling friends in Winnipeg staged a spectacular Silver Broom. Although both 1973 and 1978 were disappointing for Canada (Sweden and the USA won those events), they were pivotal in helping promote world curling. In 1973, Kjell Oscarius from Sweden defeated Regina's Harvey Mazinke, the Brier champ that year, to become the first European to win a world curling crown. In 1978, it was the turn of the USA to win, as Bob Nichols defeated Kristian Sørum of Norway in the final. The attendance that year (102,193) set an all-time record for world play that was exceeded only in 1991 when Winnipeg again hosted the Worlds.

But just as the Scotch Cup had been torpedoed from within, so too did the Air Canada Silver Broom suffer internal problems. Changes in the airline's executive suite were followed by changes in philosophy and administration. By now the ICF had become an independent body, separate from the RCCC, but largely dependent on the direction and financial support of the sponsor, Air Canada. Most of the internal changes to the event, requested by the sponsor, were accepted. But in 1984, a major, and unilateral, change was suddenly introduced, without prior notice to the participating countries.

Since the inception of the Air Canada Silver Broom, the airline had provided the same kind of benefits to competing teams as those in other major events—

Ron Northcott is the only skip to have won both a Scotch Cup (1966) and an Air Canada Silver Broom (1968 and 1969). Here's his 1969 team, from top to bottom: Northcott, third Dave Gerlach, second Bernie Sparkes, lead Fred Storey.

*Photo by Michael Burns.*

transportation, hotel expenses, daily living allowance, etc. These were paid not only to the competing teams, but also to the presidents of each of the national curling associations involved with the ICF. This assistance enabled the smaller, cash-strapped European Associations to have their presidents attend the annual ICF meeting in the host community. In Duluth that year, among a number of other changes, the presidents were suddenly told they would now have to fund their own transportation. It was a unilateral decision, with no reasons given, and was, predictably, unpopular.

Both the move itself, and the manner of the move, rankled the ICF. Two years earlier, in 1982, the international body had been presented with a hastily prepared "Sponsor's Policy" paper (shades of the Dominion Diamond D brouhaha of 1967). The paper, a surprise and embarrassment to even some of the Air Canada executives present, had been just as quickly withdrawn, and it was agreed that henceforth any changes to the sponsorship agreement would be decided through mutual discussion, not fiats from on high. In 1982, Air Canada had agreed to the discussion idea, so when the surprise announcement about presidential travel changes was made in 1984, it caused considerable concern.

At a private meeting of its executive, the federation, led by its president Clif Thompson (Canada) and supported by the ICF treasurer, and New York lawyer, Don MacKay, agreed it would advise Air Canada that it would exercise the clause in the championship contract which allowed a one-month "window" when either party could request substantive changes. The federation also outlined some "housekeeping" changes it desired. When these changes were denied by the airline, the ICF then proposed that the airline's sponsorship should cease. Privately, they hoped this somewhat Draconian move would enable a number of basic changes to be made, and the Silver Broom could be rescued from the brink. Their hopes were in vain. The new airline executives in charge of the sponsorship replied that there could be no discussion; their changes were a "take it or leave it" proposition. The ICF was forced to choose, and chose "leave it."

All this was done privately, but a number of people who had long been involved in the championship were privy to the information. When it appeared that the Silver Broom was headed for the same six-foot depth as the Scotch Cup, six of those most involved in the Silver Broom over the years formed a group called Hexagon Curling International. They prepared a confidential proposal for the ICF executive, requesting they be given the opportunity to find a replacement sponsor. In the meantime, the six (led by Chuck Hay of Scotland and Kay Sugahara of USA, plus Canadians Laurie Artiss, Don Lewis, Don Turner, and Doug Maxwell), pledged to provide the necessary funding and administration of the Worlds in an attempt to keep the event alive.

When their offer was accepted by the ICF and made public, Canada, through the CCA, objected. A subsequent full vote of the federation, at the 1984 European Championships in Morzine, France, confirmed the executive's original decision, and rejected the CCA's objections. Hexagon set out to find another sponsor.

The final Air Canada Silver Broom took place in Glasgow, Scotland, in 1985, in spite of the fact that Glasgow lacked a suitable ice facility. The committee that

When the Hexagon sponsorship contract was signed in 1985, there was an echo of the original Air Canada Silver Broom of 1967–68. The contract was signed by Chuck Hay as Hexagon president (he played in the 1968 Silver Broom), Clif Thompson (president of the ICF), and Willie Sanderson (RCCC president and former Silver Broom competitor). The contract was signed at the same table as the original 1967 contract, in the home of the Earl of Elgin, RCCC president at that time. Looking on is Doug Maxwell, Executive Director of the World Championship.

*Photo courtesy of* Canadian Curling News.

year, under the genial chairmanship of Robin Brechin, used an imaginative plan that saw a national Scottish landmark, an empty Kelvin Hall in the centre of the city, transformed magically into a curling arena, complete with spectator stands and portable ice-making plant. The final event under Air Canada support saw Canada's Al Hackner—the indomitable Iceman—win the World for the second time.

For the next three years, Hexagon attempted to find an international firm interested in sponsoring the world event. But every time a sponsor appeared set to sign a contract, mysterious mutterings were heard and somehow or other the

nascent sponsorship evaporated. After three years of searching, while sponsoring world events in Toronto, Vancouver, and Lausanne on their own, Hexagon threw in the towel.

In 1989, the ICF began to administer the world championship on its own, as the CLCA had done in earlier years with women's curling. By now, the Women's World Championship was ten years old, and the ICF made the decision to amalgamate the women's event and the men's into one championship, in Milwaukee. The event has remained twinned ever since.

It was in 1979 that the Ladies' (later Women's) World Championship was begun, in Perth, Scotland. It proved to be an immediate success. Over the next decade, and with a parade of one-year sponsorships to help fund the event, the World Women's Championship slowly built its own reputation and history. Gaby Casanova of Switzerland won the first title in 1979, and in the succeeding years of the decade, Canada won five crowns, with the others going to Sweden, Denmark, Switzerland, and Germany. By the end of the 2002 World Championships in Bismarck, North Dakota, the Canadian women had captured 12 of the 24 world titles, with the others going to Sweden (five), Switzerland and Norway (two each), Denmark, Germany, and Scotland (one apiece).

Of all the champions, two proved to be superlative, both as curlers and ambassadors of the game: Sandra Schmirler of Regina and Elizabet Gustafson of Sweden. Before her untimely death in March of 2000, Schmirler (with Jan Betker, Joan McCusker, and Marcia Gudereit) had won three world titles and an Olympic gold medal. Gustafson, a curler with the deft touch of a paediatric surgeon, which she was, led her team of Katarina Nyberg, Louise Marmont, and Elisabeth Persson to four world crowns.

During the six years from 1989 to 1994, the two World Championships survived, either with local funding, one-year sponsorships, or both. Then in

1994, a Toronto firm, the St. Clair Group, presented a marketing plan to both the CCA and the WCF (successor to the ICF). They proposed that a Season of Champions be created, embracing seven Canadian championships (Brier, Hearts, Mixed, Seniors, and Juniors), plus four world events (Men and Women, Junior Men, and Junior Women). When they introduced Ford of Canada as the new sponsor of the amalgamated World Championships (men and women), acceptance of the Season of Champions concept became a mere formality. While it would entail a different sponsorship model from the past, the difference was quickly accepted and is still in operation today.

# CHAPTER 13

# The Curse of LaBonte

**In 2002, the organizing committee of the Bismarck World Curling Championships** invited Bob LaBonte of nearby Minot, North Dakota, to be the Honourary Chairman of the 2002 Ford Worlds. He promptly asked Orest Meleschuk of Winnipeg to join him in the opening ceremonies. The two represented one of the more bizarre episodes in the history not only of the World Championships, but also of Canadian, and American, curling.

The reader will forgive me, I trust, if this becomes a first-person singular account, because I was intimately involved in the famed Curse of LaBonte. At the time, five years after the first Air Canada Silver Broom, I was Executive Director of the World Championship, and was also hosting the CBC-TV coverage of the event. In addition, I was head official at the Worlds. Remember, in those days, there was not the same emphasis put on officiating as in succeeding years. For the most part, the participating curlers were left to sort out the rules themselves, and only if they could not agree on a rule or its interpretation did they invite a local game official to get involved.

With that background and intimate involvement in the episode, I ask you, do you want the colourful story that has grown over the years? The legend of the Curse of LaBonte? Or do you want the facts? Both, you say? OK, let's go for both!

First, the facts. The Silver Broom of 1972 took place in the wonderful Bavarian resort town of Garmisch-Partenkirchen. Surrounded by the Bavarian Alps and overlooked by Germany's tallest mountain, the Zugspitze, the event had a fairy-tale quality. Warm sunshine bathed the area, and the visitors who came from all over the curling world were enchanted by it all.

In the arena, the eight teams involved (the championship would not expand to ten teams until the following year) played down till there were only two teams left, Orest Meleschuk of Canada and Bob LaBonte of the USA. Meleschuk had finished first in the round-robin preliminaries with an unbeaten record of seven wins and no losses. The USA, with a record of four wins and three losses, found itself in a four-way tie for second with Scotland (Alex Torrance), Switzerland (Peter Attinger), and Germany (Manfred Räderer). Based on the outcome of games between the tied four, and a tie-breaking game between Scotland and Switzerland, the semifinals were established. Meleschuk would play Torrance, while LaBonte would meet Räderer. Meleschuk kept his unbeaten streak going with a win over Scotland, while LaBonte beat Germany in the other semi.

The final, between Canada and the USA, started off with LaBonte making two great shots in the opening end to take a 2-0 lead. That two-point USA margin was maintained to the tenth end, when Canada had last rock advantage. Trailing 9-7, Meleshuck appeared to be on the verge of losing his first game. And the title.

The official report of the ensuing brouhaha (never before made public) put it this way.

"When Orest Meleschuk came to throw his final stone of the end, the USA had shot rock on the button, while Canada had second shot beside the US stone. The USA had third shot on the eight-foot ring, while their fourth and fifth stones were outside the eight-foot ring. Meleschuk had to remove the US 'shot' stone, and stay within the US stone on the eight-foot ring, in order to tie the game.

"His (Meleschuk's) final stone hit the US stone, passing it out of the rings, while the shooter rolled behind the tee line towards the eight-foot circle. Third Frank Aasand swept the Canadian stone vigorously onto the eight-foot ring. Aasand took a quick look at the Canadian rock, and then the US rock to determine which was second shot. He quickly threw his hands in the air [see photo 1, p.169] to signal that, in his opinion, the USA was victorious.

"It was a unilateral action and did not involve third Dave Romano of the Canadian side, who had not yet looked at the Canadian stone (see photos 1 and 2). Romano . . . presumably would decide whether he wished a measure or would concede defeat. At no time during those final moments did he look at his own stone. Nor did he offer to shake hands, conceding defeat. Until Romano did so (according to Rule 16), the game was not over.

"As soon as Aasand had thrown his hands in the air, skip Bob LaBonte came into the house, dancing a small jig (photo 2). He threw his broom in the air and jumped off the ice. As he landed, his feet slipped from under him (photo 3) and his right foot kicked the Canadian stone tangentially from its original resting position to a new position, still on the eight-foot circle. At almost the same time, Aasand reached for LaBonte's right foot (photo 3).

"All of this happened with surprising speed. The total elapsed time, from the moment the Canadian rock stopped moving until it was kicked, amounted to six seconds. The Canadian third (Romano) indicated he thought the US had kicked the Canadian stone. . . . In the next few minutes, neither Aasand nor LaBonte reported that the Canadian stone had been touched.

"There is no provision in the rules [remember, this was in 1972] whereby the umpire may indicate whether or not an infraction has been committed, and in any event it is not up to the umpire to declare a burned rock. That responsibility (in both the rules and etiquette) belongs to the players involved. When neither Aasand nor LaBonte indicated the stone had been burned, this was reported to Romano."

All this, with thirty years of hindsight, is—and was—understandable. LaBonte could not have felt the slight brush of the stone by his foot when he was smarting from the jolt of his ungainly landing on the ice.

There was another unfortunate aspect to the situation, never revealed before now. Originally, the CBC-TV crew had planned to bring a compact TV unit (designed for special use during Canada's Centennial year) to Germany. They had just recently developed the replay and slow-motion capability taken so much for granted today, and it would have been invaluable in sorting out exactly what happened. But a labour dispute in Canada cancelled its use, and so there was no instant replay capability on hand!

The sequence of the famous "kicked rock caper" in Garmisch-Partenkirchen, 1972.

*Photos by Michael Burns*

**#1:** Frank Aasand of the USA (in white) signals what he thinks is victory. Dave Romano of Canada (in dark) looks at the USA stone to check its exact location, before looking at the Canadian stone. Bob LaBonte is in the rear, at the hack.

**#2:** LaBonte moves into the rings, where he loses his footing, after jumping in the air. Romano is still checking the USA stone on the eight-foot ring.

**# 3:** LaBonte lands on his back, as Aasand reaches for his foot. Romano has yet to check the Canadian rock's position. The entire sequence took only six seconds.

"Nobody had a better view of the LaBonte incident than I did from my seat on the media bench. I still recall the gasp in the arena and voices shouting, 'He kicked it.' The amazing thing to me is the stone only moved about a foot after LaBonte kicked it, and he barely altered its position in relation to the 8-foot ring. I remember interviewing Frank Aasand after-wards. I told him he was the only person in the world who might make a judgement on the two stones, and what did he think. He replied, 'It was close, and might have required a measure anyway, but I thought we had it.'

Years later, in Duluth [1984], I talked to LaBonte, who told me 'In 1972, I got over the disappointment fairly quickly. I was young, and thought I'd be back a bunch of times to win the Worlds. Now it's harder to take, because I'm beginning to realize I'll never get another chance.'

The other thing I remember about the incident was Orest's final stone of the extra end. What a beauty it was, diving into the four-foot behind cover. LaBonte couldn't follow it and that was the game. Meleschuk won the world without a loss, but it sure was close."

—*Bob Picken*

If the stone had been declared a burned rock by the USA, Canada would have been given the benefit of placement, and no measure would have been made. The game would have been ruled a tie, and an extra end would have been required. In the absence of any admission or corroboration of the kicked stone, however, it was ruled that the stone could not be considered a burned rock. When a measure was requested, it showed that Canada had the necessary two points to tie the game.

Back to the official report for the summary: "In the extra end, LaBonte (with last rock advantage) was unable to match the final draw that Meleschuk deliv-ered. When LaBonte's last stone slid through the rings, leaving Canada with shot rock in the four-foot circle, the Air Canada Silver Broom was awarded to Canada by a score of 10-9."

Those are the facts. But with such a story, unmatched in the history of the game, all kinds of embroidery have been added in the intervening years. The USA team officials felt that they had been robbed of a championship. Canadians were equally convinced they had been made to appear ungracious in victory for something that was completely outside their control. Everybody present (and that number has grown exponentially in the intervening years!) can relate their own

When Rick Folk's Canadian team received the Air Canada Silver Broom and champion's banner from President Claude Taylor in 1980, it was said that Canada had finally exorcised "The Curse of LaBonte." From l-r are Ron Mills, Rick Folk, Taylor, Tom Wilson, and Jim Wilson.
*Photo by Michael Burns.*

version of the story, and depending on their allegiance, point out that the USA could—or should—have won it in the extra end.

It wasn't until much later that "The Curse of LaBonte" was revealed. One of Canada's more inventive and colourful journalists, Larry Tucker, is generally given credit for inventing the hex. According to Tucker's flight of fancy, it was as if LaBonte had sworn an oath that for the next seven years no Canadian (later changed to no Manitoban) team would win a world title. If the "curse" had been revealed in 1972, the story would have taken on a life of its own and grown immensely over the ensuing years. It would have made a good story even better, indeed sensational. But that never happened.

What did happen was that in the ensuing years, such outstanding Canadian teams as those led by Harvey Mazinke, Hector Gervais, Bill Tetley, Jack MacDuff, Jim Ursel, Ed Lukowich, and Barry Fry all failed to win gold. It wasn't until the

1980 Silver Broom in Moncton that Canada, under Rick Folk, was able to clamber back onto the winner's podium.

The explanation of Canada's seven-year drought at the Worlds was more easily explained by the "curse" than by the rapidly improving quality of play by the world's smaller curling countries. To be accurate, "The Curse of LaBonte" was Larry Tucker's wonderfully fanciful description of how it was that Folk was able to win the 1980 Silver Broom: It was the seven-year hex, Tucker wrote, and it had run its course!

Today, "The Curse of LaBonte" is one of the more colourful chapters in the story of the World Championships. And the "celebration" of the curse, thirty years later, in Bismarck, with the two central figures present, only added to the aura—and the memory—of the event.

# CHAPTER 14

# Curling and the Olympics

**Although there had been world championship curling since 1959, it wasn't until** 1966 that the International Curling Federation was formed, as a committee of the Royal Caledonian Curling Club. In 1982, the ICF became independent, recognized as the governing body for world curling. In 1991, the name was changed to the World Curling Federation.

Ever since its formation, the International Curling Federation had talked of having curling recognized as an Olympic sport. There was a naïve assumption that once the International Olympic Committee realized curling's traditions and appeals, which mirrored, and seemed eminently compatible with, Olympic ideals, then the sport would gain an easy and welcome entry into the five-rings family.

The first real move to curry Olympic favour began with Clif Thompson, the Canadian president of the ICF from 1982–85, when he met with IOC president, Juan Antonio Samaranch, in December 1984 in Lausanne, Switzerland. While Samaranch appeared receptive to the ICF, he was also noncommittal. Thompson's successor, Philip Dawson of Scotland, continued the lobbying, and there were high hopes that with a successful demonstration of curling at the Calgary Games of 1988, entry to the Olympics as a full-fledged medal sport would be as easy as a hogged rock. After all, the ICF had a stunning record of over twenty-five years of world championship play to buttress its bid.

It fell to Calgary's Ray Kingsmith, a past president of the CCA and a long-time media personality, to become the prime organizer of the curling events at the '88 Games. Although Kingsmith and his cohorts organized the curling to showcase the sport to the Olympic officials in attendance, and although tickets for the event sold out early, and although the knowledgeable fans in the Max Bell Arena were enthusiastic, the IOC didn't take the bait. It began to dawn on the world of curling that entry into the Olympics was perhaps more a political matter than a sporting one.

According to IOC regulations, curling would need a minimum of 25 participating countries, from three of the five world continents, before it could be welcomed into the Olympic Family. It didn't matter that the regulations had been overlooked before (and would be again) for other "ice and snow" events to gain admission. So curling went back to square one and set out, once again, to gain favourable notice from the rest of the Olympic world. The ICF (rechristened as the World Curling Federation to avoid confusion with the International Canoeing Federation) set about to meet the IOC requirements.

Led by president Gunther Hummelt of Austria, the WCF recruited new curling countries regardless of their curling size or proficiency. Such hitherto unknown curling hotbeds as Andorra, Mexico, the US Virgin Islands, Hungary, and Bulgaria, to name but a few, became WCF members. Together with the older curling communities of the world—Canada, Scotland, the USA, Sweden, Switzerland, Germany, Norway, and the like—the WCF soon reached the magic number of 25 countries. But they didn't stop there. By the 2002 Winter Games, the WCF boasted a total of 36 curling countries (a 37th, China, would be added a month later). Some of these countries even had ice, rocks, hacks, and a handful of curlers!

If Hummelt was the high-profile leader in the bid for medal-sport recognition, there were two others who proved equally invaluable to the cause. Franz

Tanner was a former world championship curler, for Switzerland, but, more importantly, he was well and favourably known among Olympic officials in his hometown of Lausanne, where the IOC had its headquarters. It was Tanner, whose personal friendship with Juan Antonio Samaranch and other high Olympic officials was vital, who gave curling its major boost. And from Canada, there was a knowledgeable backroom Olympian—Jack Lynch—who became the *éminence grise* in helping to smooth the way with his pertinent advice. Lynch, a long-time technical director of the Canadian Olympic Association, possessed a broad knowledge of all things Olympian. The WCF eagerly sought, and Lynch willingly offered, that background and knowledge. Nor did it hurt that Lynch himself was an avid curler in his hometown of St. Bruno, Quebec.

Most observers thought that once the necessary statistical requirements were met, curling's acceptance as a member of the Olympic Family would be virtually automatic. They soon found out it wasn't that easy. They would have to gain a favourable vote from the ninety-odd individual member nations of the IOC. And before that, any recommendation to the IOC Executive for medal status would have to be filtered through the Programme Commission, two of whose members, Canadian skier Ken Read, and the Russian chairman, Vitaly Smirnov, were opposed to the idea. And lurking behind a variety of subterfuges, seldom, if ever, mentioned in public, were the implications of the almighty dollar.

By now, the increasingly large revenues from the sale of television rights, primarily to major US networks, were being divided among the IOC, the host organizing committee, and the six participating winter Olympic sports. There was no financial problem when a new event, inside an existing sport, was added

**Jack Lynch.**

*Photo courtesy* Canadian Curling News.

to the Games. Short track speed skating, for example, was considered a part of the existing sport of speed skating, so its addition to the roster of competitions was quick and easy because it made no difference in the split of television money. But curling, as a new sport, would necessitate a redistribution of that money. What had formerly been divvied up into six would now have to be split seven ways, and that was a major hurdle in getting curling accepted as a medal sport.

The "favourable notice" the WCF had coveted for so many years finally came, in Barcelona, in July 1992. The IOC announced that curling would be a definite addition to the 2002 Winter Games, and a negotiable addition to the 1998 Winter Olympics, depending on which city won the bid for '98. It should be noted that, in a related move, the IOC had switched the years of the Winter Games so they would occur midway through the four-year Olympiade, with Lillehammer, Norway, originally slated for 1996, advanced to 1994. Although the Norwegians had originally indicated a desire to include curling as a demonstration sport, it was turned down when the IOC ruled against any further demonstration events after 1992.

When Nagano, Japan, was chosen as the site for the 1998 Winter Games, curlers were happy, for Nagano had earlier said it would include curling in its schedule. The curling portion of the '98 Games was held in Karuizawa, and with "proper" medals on the line, there was enhanced excitement over curling. Curling fans were entranced by the prospect of their heroes winning Olympic medals; the World Curling Federation was entranced by the prospect of funding beyond their wildest dreams. Both dreams became reality. Canada's Sandra Schmirler foursome won gold; the Mike Harris team won silver. And the WCF gained US $3.8 million dollars—about $6 million Canadian—from its share of

the television rights fees. (More about Canada and Olympic curling appears in the next chapter.)

Since curling's entry into the Olympics, there have been a variety of formats used to determine the winners of gold, silver, and bronze. In Chamonix, 1924, there was no women's curling, and only three countries showed up for a series of 18-end games. In Lake Placid, in 1932, Canada's four teams played the USA's four teams. There were no playoffs, and no women's teams were present. In Calgary 1988, women's teams competed for the first time. The format this time was a round-robin preliminary series, followed by a three-country playoff.

In France in 1992, when curling was again a demonstration sport, arena difficulties in Pralognan la Vanoise, near the main Olympic city of Albertville, forced organizers to put the eight teams into two four-country groups. A preliminary round-robin in each group decided which two teams would then go to a "cross-over" playoff in which the leader in Group A played the second-place team in Group B, and vice versa. The 1992 decision that brought curling into full membership in the Olympics also agreed that the best form of competition for 1998 in Japan would be an eight-team preliminary round-robin followed by a four-team playoff.

In 2002, the number of teams was increased to ten in both the men's and women's events. Four-team playoffs followed the round-robin, but because the arena in Ogden was configured for only four sheets of ice (for TV purposes), only eight teams could play at any one time (the other two teams would draw a bye). As a result, it took almost two weeks of play before the medals were handed out.

No matter what format was used, there was the constant of gold, silver, and bronze waiting at the end.

# CHAPTER 15

# Canada's Olympic Past

**If Canada mined Olympic silver and bronze in February 2002, while seeking** gold, then it would be fair to say that the mining of those metals began about 240 years earlier. Those "miners" of the eighteenth century may not have been the lineal forebears of Kelley Law and Kevin Martin and their teams, but they most certainly were their spiritual forebears. Not only could Canada's Olympic curlers sing their praises, but thousands of Canadians could also join the gratitude chorus, for those first Scots who came to Canada loved the game and their new country so much that it would become the greatest curling nation in the world. That's "greatest," as in "the most curlers," "the best curlers," "the widest range of curlers," "the most innovative curlers." Use whatever objective yardstick you wish, Canada is by far the largest curling country in the world—more curlers than the other 35 WCF member countries combined. Canada is also the most successful curling country in the world, having won more world championships and trophies than any other country. That the second should flow from the first is no mystery; in a country that boasts over a million curlers, it is only natural that the best of the bunch should be world-class.

But while the World Curling Championships have consistently proved that Canada is "best in class," it is a different story at the Olympics. Canadian curlers,

Canada's first Olympic curling heroes were the winners of the 1932 curling competition in Lake Placid. The un-beaten Winnipeg team consisted of (l-r) Errick Willis, Robert Pow, James Bowman, and William Burns (skip).

*Photo courtesy Western Canada Pictorial Index, #A2404-71569.*

both men and women, have been quite inconsistent at the Winter Games, whether competing in a medal event or a demonstration event.

Canada's first Olympic curlers journeyed to the Lake Placid Games in 1932, when the world was still recovering from the great Wall Street crash of 1929. Many countries could not afford to send full teams of winter athletes—the main criteria for the inclusion of curling teams in Lake Placid was the willingness of players to pay their own way. Canada and the USA each had four curling teams. Canada was represented by foursomes from Manitoba, Ontario, Northern Ontario, and Quebec, while the USA sent teams from Connecticut, New York,

**The gold medal won by the Winnipeg curling team in 1932 at the Lake Placid Winter Olympics shows an Olympic maiden (with trumpet) surmounted by the five Olympic rings on the front; and on the obverse are intricate carvings of six "official" sports (clockwise from eight o'clock—hockey, figure skating, ski jumping, nordic skiing, speed skating and bob sled). Curling is depicted bottom left, while the bottom right image appears to be dog-sled racing!**

*Errick Willis' champion's medal courtesy of Errick Willis Jr.*
*Photograph by Richard McNaughton.*

Massachusetts, and Michigan. Each Canadian team played each American team. Canada won 12 of the 16 games; the USA won four. The Manitoba team, the only one with a perfect 4-0 record, was recognized as the gold medal team. It was skipped by William Burns, and included lead Errick Willis (a later Lieutenant-Governor of Manitoba), Robert Pow at second, and James Bowman at third. The games were played on outdoor ice and, in later years, Willis would recall that on a couple of occasions, they had to wait to practise until the darling of the day, figure skater Sonja Henie, had finished using the ice!

The next time curling surfaced as an Olympic (demonstration) sport was in 1988, in Calgary. Eight countries sent their best teams, the event was superbly organized, and tickets sold out early. The only problem was that the bulk of those early tickets had been snapped up by multinational corporations bent on using them as entertainment freebies for special customers. If they went unused, the companies didn't much care, and so while there were curling fans outside the Max Bell Arena clamouring to get in, the box office had to tell them that there were no tickets available! That situation lasted for only a couple of days. High-level meetings were held, and it was agreed to sell rush tickets for any seats unoccupied after two ends of play.

The 1988 event was a seven-game, round-robin series followed by a three-team playoff. When the women's event was over, Canada's Linda Moore team, with Lindsay Sparkes, Debbie Jones-Walker, Penny Ryan, and Patti Vande, wore the women's gold medals. Moore had finished the round-robin series in second place, and went on to defeat third-place

Canada won its first modern-day Olympic gold medal in curling in 1988, when curling was still a demonstration sport. The Calgary winners were (l-r) Linda Moore, Lindsay Sparkes, Debbie Jones-Walker, Penny Ryan and Patti Vande.

*Canadian Olympic Committee photo courtesy Canadian Curling Association.*

Norway (Dordi Nordby) in the semi-final. Then in the final Canada downed first-place Sweden, led by Elisabeth Hogström. The gold in curling was one of just three gold medals overall for Canada, all in demonstration events (curling, freestyle skiing, and short track speed skating). In the official medal events, Canada came up empty-handed. When Calgary produced a profit from its Winter Games, much of the money was ploughed back into the Calgary Olympic Development Association (CODA) and has been used since to help develop Canada's Olympic potential.

The men did not fare as well. There was no question that Canada's best team was in place for 1988. Canada's 1986 Brier and World championship team of Ed Lukowich, John Ferguson, Neil Houston, Brent Syme, and Wayne Hart finished the round-robin tied for the top (five wins, two losses) with Switzerland. But the Swiss team, led by Hansjurg Lips, was ranked number one, having beaten Canada in their preliminary game, and the Swiss thus gained a bye to the final.

In the semifinal, the Canadians lost to Eigil Ramsfjell of Norway, who had survived a two-game tie-breaking series with Sweden (Dan Ola Ericksson) and the USA (Bud Somerville). Norway went on to defeat Switzerland for the gold medal. The bronze medal was scant consolation for Lukowich and Canada. A month later, Ramsfjell completed an international sweep by defeating Canada's Pat Ryan in the World Championship final in Lausanne, Switzerland.

Canada was looking for redemption in the Albertville Games of 1992, in the idyllic mountain setting of Pralognan la Vanoise. But that was all that was idyllic for the curlers. Two of the four sheets of ice were virtually unplayable, while the other two left much to be desired. In addition, there were organizational and administrative problems. The result was a nightmare for Canada. The newly minted Free Guard Zone, established in 1991, was used in international curling for the first time, and although a few of the Europeans had some experience with it, it was all new to the Canadians. Instead of playing a full, eight-team round-robin series, the countries were divided into two groups, with playoffs taking place between the top teams of each group. Canada was represented by its two 1991 national champions, Kevin Martin and Julie Sutton. Although both Canadian teams made the playoffs, Martin lost his semifinal game, and the ensuing bronze medal game, and finished fourth, out of the medals, while Sutton dropped her semifinal game, but won bronze. The men's gold medal went to Urs Dick of Switzerland; the women's gold was won by Andrea Schöpp of Germany.

There was general unhappiness, in 1992, over the curling. If one of the main benefits of an Olympic experience is the chance to play all the other teams

**The Sandra Schmirler team, complete with flowers and gold medals, in 1998. l–r, Atina Ford, Marcia Gudereit, Joan McCusker, Jan Betker, and Sandra Schmirler.**

*Photo courtesy Jim Waite.*

present, then everybody got short-changed. It was agreed that things would have to change for the next Winter Games.

Those next games took place in 1998, in Nagano, Japan. The competition, for both men's and women's, still involved eight countries, who played a full round-robin series, followed this time by a four-team playoff. In Karuizawa, where the curling took place, Canada was represented by a relatively unknown team of men, skipped by Mike Harris of Toronto, while the women were led by three-time Canadian and World winner, Sandra Schmirler of Regina. And for the first time, with curling recognized as a full Olympic medal sport, they were playing for "real" gold.

Canadians from coast to coast to coast were thrilled as they watched the action. And watch they did. Even though the time difference between Japan and Canada meant they had to watch the games in the middle of the night, Canadian fans did so, some organizing midnight bonspiels to help them stay awake to watch their heroes.

Even the weather helped out! The fog that settled over the Nagano ski hills meant that most of the ski events had to be postponed, then rescheduled. But curling, always available for the cameras, received blanket television coverage.

But if the weather helped the curling, the flu bug did not. Influenza roared through the Olympic village, forcing some seriously affected competitors to be air-lifted to hospital. Sandra Schmirler's team, Jan Betker, Joan McCusker, Marcia Gudereit, and alternate Atina Ford, suffered early in the week. When

**Mike Hay of Scotland exults in a shot well-made in 1986, when playing Canada's Ed Lukowich in the Toronto World Championship.**
*Photo by Michael Burns.*

Betker was forced to withdraw, Ford moved in smoothly and efficiently. And when it came time for the playoffs, the Schmirler foursome, now fully recovered, were in top form. They edged Britain's Kirsty Hay in the semis and then downed Denmark's Helena Blach Lavrsen in the final for the gold medal. One gold medal was in safekeeping; the script now called for a last-day drive for a second gold. Cue Mike Harris, who had finished the preliminary series in first place with his team of Richard Hart, Collin Mitchell, George Karrys, and alternate Paul Savage.

But the illness that the men had evaded throughout the week had other plans for the playoffs. In his semifinal, Skip Mike Harris ran a temperature of

101°F, but still curled magnificently, as Canada downed the USA's Tim Somerville. That put Canada into the final against Switzerland's Patrick Hurlimann, who had beaten Norway's hero of a decade earlier, Eigil Ramsfjell, in the other semifinal.

On that final day Canada was faced with a no-win situation. Harris's temperature by now had soared to 103°F, and there was deep concern in the Canadian camp. Should they shunt Harris aside and move Paul Savage into the driver's seat? Savage, an experienced skip with impeccable credentials, had thrown only two stones in preliminary play—enough to qualify for a medal. After working so hard and so long to reach this point, Harris desperately wanted to play. It wasn't a hard decision for the team; Harris had earned his chance to shoot for the top. Privately, team officials were hoping he'd be able to come close to his 92 percent semifinal shooting mark.

In the best fictional tradition of the old Frank Merriwell sports sagas, or in the world of Hollywood, Harris would have emerged triumphant in the final end, and then collapsed into his fans' waiting arms. But Karuizawa didn't know Frank Merriwell from Frank Ne'er Do Well. While the rest of the team played magnificently, Harris collapsed (figuratively) early in the game and finished with a shocking 25 percent shooting mark—less than a quarter the size of his raging temperature. In racetrack terms, Hurlimann won, going away. Canada had to settle for silver.

Canada's joy when the Sandra Schmirler team won the first official gold medal in curling's Olympic history was short-lived. Within eighteenth months, Schmirler would succumb to cancer, leaving behind a husband, two young daughters, and a grieving nation. The memory of the three-time world winner and gold medal champion skip is perpetuated in the Sandra Schmirler Foundation, set up to assist Canadian families whose children face life-threatening diseases.

# CHAPTER 16

# Curling's Special Events and Special People

## Morning Classes

Among the esoterica of curling is something called "Morning Classes," or, when he was alive, "Collie's Classes." Today, it's just "Classes."

You must understand that, first of all, they aren't classes in the schoolroom sense. They have nothing to do with pedagogical pursuits. They are educational only in the broadest sense. But they have been a part of modern curling since the end of World War II. They are an integral part of the Brier (whether Macdonald, Labatt, or Nokia), and to a lesser extent, the World Curling Championships. They are not found in any of the other major curling events of the land.

So what are Morning Classes? In two words, gin collins.

Every morning during the Canadian Curling Championships, and sometimes the Worlds, sundry fans gather in a hotel room from 7:00 to 9:00 a.m. to sip freshly squeezed lemon juice, soda water, and sugar—with a splash of gin, if that's your preference. It's a place to go to meet people, to hear the latest curling gossip, to grimace at the tartness of the lemons; in short, to participate in the camaraderie of curling.

So how did they start? Why were they called Collie's Classes? How essential are they to the survival of the sport?

The answers are easy. Gather round, class, and pay attention. Or not, if you like. There are no exams after. Collie would be Colin A. Campbell, one-time Brier competitor (1951), an early president of the CCA (1947–48), and subsequently a Brier trustee (from 1965 to his death on Christmas Day, 1978, at the age of 77). For a number of years (1969–79) he was president of the ICF, and he was also one of just two Honourary Life Members of the RCCC—Prince Philip being the other. He was a Liberal politician and a mining engineer from Northern Ontario and, at one time, was a cabinet minister in the Ontario government under Premier Mitchell Hepburn. He was, it is safe to say, one of the giants of Canadian and world curling.

When World War II erupted, Britain needed hard rock miners to work on the defences of Gibraltar. Collie Campbell resigned his government post to become a brigadier in the Canadian Army. His task was to get the fortifications of Gibraltar finished quickly and efficiently. "Mining hogs" from the hard rock mining communities in Northern Ontario and Quebec were recruited into the army and set to work around the clock, 24 hours a day, 7 days a week.

In order to obtain maximum efficiency and co-ordination, staff meetings were held every morning at 6:00 a.m. But after the initial enthusiasm abated, and with the heavy work schedule, attendance at the meetings suffered. Several ideas were implemented to improve the attendance; none worked. One day, Brigadier Campbell ordered all hands to appear the next day for "a pleasant surprise." The pleasant surprise was a gin collins for everyone, whether they were coming off the night shift or just getting ready to head underground. The "pleasant surprise," every morning, seemed to work. Attendance remained high, and the mining efforts continued apace. After the war, when Campbell became president of the DCA in 1947, "Collie's Classes" were continued, in a different context. Whether by design or good fortune, they became Colin Campbell's

**Morning Classes were always well attended when the Hon. Colin Campbell presided and provided some distilled curling wisdom.**
*Photo by Michael Burns.*

**Morning Classes were always well attended when the Hon. Colin Campbell presided and provided some distilled curling wisdom.**
*Photo by Michael Burns.*

power base. He was an unparalleled politician, in the best sense of the word, and many a touchy curling subject was settled in amicable fashion at Classes.

Initially only for members of the curling executive and curlers, the early morning gathering became a popular rendezvous, assumed a life of its own, and has continued to this day. Throughout most of its curling life, the morning eye-opener relied for its success on two ingredients: willing volunteer helpers and enthusiastic "students." The volunteer helpers were, for the most part, fellow curlers from Northern Ontario. They were the ones to help—mainly with the squeezing of countless dozens of lemons. The "students" were any curling fans willing to arise early enough and stay late enough (classes began at 7:00 a.m. and finished at 9:00 a.m.)to enjoy meeting new friends and exchange early-

**The logo of the Friars' Briar.**

*Courtesy of Rev. Wilfred Raths.*

THE FRIARS'

BRIAR

morning gossip. It was also an unwritten rule that each student, or couple, would contribute a bottle of gin to the classroom. During the Silver Broom years, it was the sponsor who contributed the essential ingredients.

After Campbell's death, his Northern Ontario friends and his daughter, June Perry, made sure the Classes were continued. They serve as an equally important memorial to a remarkable curler, as does the Colin A. Campbell Memorial Award, in World Curling. More on the latter, later.

### The Friars' Briar

Very few, if any, of Canada's major sports are so connected to the clergy as is curling. Almost every provincial association has its chaplain. The first visit of Scots to Canada had the Rev. John Kerr, historian and curler, as its captain. The early minutes of many clubs record that the Rev. Whoever "would be accorded a complimentary membership in the club," and in the latter half of the twentieth century, an annual Friars' Briar was begun, at which clergy curlers from all across the country could gather in collegial competition. The fact that it occasionally (well, OK, more than occasionally) took place in the same locality, and at the same time, as the Macdonald, Labatt, or Nokia Brier is purely coincidental.

For many years an opening feature of the Brier or the Tournament of Hearts was the non-denominational Church Parade, and if sometimes the parade turned out to be less successful than normally, that was OK too. Robin Wilson, co-ordinator of the Scott Tournament of Hearts, recalls that in 1982, the chair of the organizing committee had chosen (with great care) a minister who would handle the non-denominational church service, "and how was she to know he would preach a sermon on circumcision!"

Nor should one think that because they were clergy they were somehow or other slackers on the ice. The Reverend Guy Scholz, Lutheran minister and author of the book *Gold on Ice: The Story of the Sandra Schmirler Curling Team*, affirms that many members of the clergy are, by nature, competitive. It may be a "quieter form of competitiveness, in the sense (we) are competing with many other alternatives in our community, in a battle of souls, trying to sell people on a better or healthier way of life." When he made that statement, perhaps Scholz had in mind the famous W. O. Mitchell play, *The Black Bonspiel of Willie MacCrimmon*, a recasting of the Faustian legend into the curling rink. The play has been a staple of curling communities for many years.

Scholz echoes the words of many ministers who, when asked why curling and the clergy have been linked since the game's beginnings, point to the fact that in many communities in the 1900s, the curling rink was the social hub of the town or village. If, as a new pastor, you wanted to be a part of the community (and you did, of course) you learned to curl. Also, curling's emphasis on etiquette may have held a stronger appeal than some of the more physical pastimes that focused on bulk and brute strength.

In Winnipeg, there has been a Chaplains Curling Club for more than fifty years, but many of its more devoted members are at a loss to provide historical details. The Rev. Wilfred K. Raths reports that he has been a member for over fifty years, has twice served as president of the club, has played in the mammoth Manitoba Bonspiel from 1948 to 1998, but is unaware whether or not there is a club constitution.

"At the Annual Meeting," reports Mr. Raths, in a personal letter, "the minutes are never read. Someone always moves that the minutes be accepted as recorded." For ministers, who must deal daily with many and various committees, with their many and varied minutes, the chance to accept the minutes at the club's annual meeting, "as recorded," must hold a special allure. Raths goes on to say that, "During my half century with the club, the majority of its members were from the following denominations (in order of numbers): United, Lutheran, Anglican, Presbyterian, Mennonite, Baptist, Roman Catholic, Unitarian, Church of Christ, Salvation Army, Nazarene, one Rabbi and occasionally a non-denominational clergyman. It is," he concludes, "the most ecumenical organization I have ever had the privilege of belonging to, where honour, respect and sportsmanship is paramount."

### The Hawksnest Club

Originally a fishing club based in Oshawa, many of the Hawksnesters were curlers who came annually to the Brier in its early days. As volunteers, they were pressed into service as record keepers, scorekeepers, and occasionally as umpires. All they asked for was a chance to be alongside the great curlers of the land. One of their badges of office was a dress Stewart tartan jacket. The only way you could be invited to become a member of the club was to wait for a death in the group, and then be invited to don the deceased's tartan jacket. Sleeves too long, or too short? Too bad—you're now a member. And you don't have to wear the jacket too often anyway. One of their delights was an annual luncheon at the Brier, that two or three media friends would be invited to attend. No one ever turned down the invitation.

## The ACSBPHAICBJS

In the early days of the Air Canada Silver Broom, there was a feeling among the organizers that while much was being done for the players and officials (free transportation and hotel accommodation, daily living allowance, complimentary tickets to all the social events, etc.) little was done for the fans who followed their teams to the WCC each year. Most of them flew on Air Canada jets to attend the event, and so helped the commercial side of the sponsor. In addition, they spent a fair amount of money to buy tickets, hotel accommodation, meals, and souvenirs at the host site, and there was a feeling that such fans deserved to be more than mere spectators. In a very real sense, they were considered important participants in the annual event. They helped give "the Broom" its special flavour. Out of this feeling grew the opinion that a special club should be formed.

Enter the ACSBPHAICBJS—the Air Canada Silver Broom Pond Hoppers And International Curling Buff Jet Set—a club that had just one membership requirement. To become a Pond Hopper, one only had to arrive at the event by crossing an ocean (Atlantic or Pacific), or, in the vernacular of the day, by hopping the pond. Having done that, each member was given a special scroll detailing their membership number, and, in a droll manner, their "obligations."

When Air Canada ceased its sponsorship of the WCC, the name was changed to the NARPHAICBJS (the New And Revised Pond Hoppers etc., etc.). Today it is familiarly known as the Pond Hopper Club, and with leadership from within, is an integral part of each year's Ford World Curling Championships. By the turn of the century, the number of Pond Hoppers had reached the 10,000 mark.

**Brier Bear (aka Reg Caughie).**

*Photo by Diane Caughie.*

## Brier Bear

In 1981, a year after the Brier had changed its sponsorship from Macdonald Tobacco to Labatt Breweries, the organizing committee in Halifax was looking for a way to help promote its event. The suggestion was made that perhaps a mascot would be useful. So one of the committee members volunteered to don an outfit and appear at shopping malls, curling clubs, wherever, to help promote the '81 Brier. It was meant to be a short-term job, but as so often happens, Brier Bear became an integral part of the 1981 Brier. And the 1982 event. And also 1983.

Reg Caughie, the original volunteer, soon became a fixture that helped make the Labatt Brier a worthy successor to the Macdonald Brier. His gentle idiosyncrasies never interfered with the action on the ice. His appearance at Children's Hospitals and at other charity events, helped the legend grow. In 2005, Caughie will celebrate twenty-five years of his original, temporary, short-term job!

**When the Skins Game was held in Barrie, ON, in 2001, the originators of the event, Jim Thompson (left) of TSN and the author (right), reminisced about the event's inaugural days in 1986.**

*Photo courtesy* Canadian Curling News.

## The Skins Game

In the mid-1980s, curling ice at the Brier and other major events had become so good, and the top curlers of the land had become so proficient at the takeout game, that matches became deadly dull and boring. The less-than-elegant peel game had become so prevalent that final scores of 4–3, 3–2 and 2–1 were becoming more and more common. Few fans enjoyed a succession of blank ends, and television in particular found the dreary parade of low scores off-putting.

So when TSN vice-president Jim Thompson and the author were commiserating over the direction curling appeared to be heading, they next wondered what might be done to enhance the game. Out of these conversations came curling's version of the golf Skins Game. As projected, each end of a game would become a game in itself. Money would be set as a prize for each end played, but could only be won in either of two ways. The team holding last rock advantage (the hammer) could win only if it could score two or more points in the end. The team without the hammer could cash in by winning the end ("stealing the end" in curling terms). If the end were blanked, or if the hammer team could only score one point, the money at stake would be carried over to the next end. The game would be won not by points scored but by the team that won the most money.

The first TSN Skins game was held in Newmarket, Ontario, in 1986, and involved a star-studded lineup of four former Brier and World champions: Ed Lukowich, Ed Werenich, Rick Folk, and Al Hackner. In addition to the money at stake ($30,000), the teams were put under the pressure of having to finish the game within a prescribed time limit. This part of the Skins—time clocks—was new at the time and arose out of research that had been ongoing since 1983. The Skins Game proved an instant hit with viewers, and when the giant New Brunswick company, McCain Foods (Canada), became involved in 1989 as sponsor and guiding force, it became a yearly "must-watch" television event that combined huge prize monies and top teams.

### The Sports Network and Gordon Craig

Perhaps that heading should read Gordon Craig and TSN, for while not many curlers know Gordon Craig by name, they do by reputation. If there is any one person who has helped Canadian curling grow and prosper, through the power of television, that man is Gordon Craig.

Born in Brandon, and brought up in Winnipeg, he attended university for a year, but then decided it was not for him. When he quit college after one year, infuriating his father, he took a job in the mailroom of the CBC. In true Horatio Alger fashion, he moved from the mailroom into the TV studio, from there into TV production and thence to the executive suite. Eventually he became one of Canada's most knowledgeable experts on sport and television, with a string of "firsts" to his credit, including television's first coverage of curling; first wall-to-wall Olympic coverage anywhere; first president of the 24-hour-a-day sports channel, TSN.

In 1962, when the Kitchener Brier ended in a three-way tie (Ernie Richardson, Norm Houck, and Hector Gervais), it was Craig who moved quickly to bring a mobile truck and three cameras from Toronto down the highway to Kitchener to cover the final playoff live.

**Gordon Craig, curling's best television friend, receives yet another award.**

*Photo by Michael Burns.*

He was the first broadcast executive to see the potential of curling on television, and he brought a series of great curling events to the small screen (CBC Championship Curling, the Brier, and Silver Broom). He left the CBC to start TSN in 1984, where he became its first president, and he built it from a single entity with 50 employees in Toronto, into four separate television companies employing over 750 across Canada.

When the original owner of TSN, Labatts, was itself sold, to the Belgian brewing giant, Interbrew, Canadian regulations forced the sale of TSN, and Craig spearheaded a Canadian group that bought the network (for $605 million), renaming the new operation Netstar Communications. Just prior to retiring as chairman and CEO of Netstar, he masterminded its sale to the CTV Network, from whence it was acquired by Bell Globemedia.

Throughout his career, curling was one of his major passions. His recognition of curling as one of Canada's sporting jewels has helped give Canadian (and world) curling events a prominence unlike any other.

## The Canadian Curling Hall of Fame and Museum

Canada's Curling Hall of Fame and Museum has had more ups and downs than a yo-yo contest. And while it has existed for over twenty-five years, it is curling's version of L'il Orphan Annie. In 1983, when Tom Fisher was president of the CCA, and his wife Anne was deeply involved in curling in Montreal, both became integral parts of an attempt to find a permanent site for the Hall of Fame. The Hall had been formally established by vote of the CCA in 1972, but its only site in all that time was the Fisher's basement and garage in Baie D'Urfe, a suburb of Montreal. Thirty years later, the Hall of Fame and Museum's accumulated memorabilia, photos and pins are still in need of a permanent site. While there are a number of provincial Halls of Fame, there is, as yet, no national building where curling's greatest memories can be exhibited properly.

Over the years, the CCA made a number of attempts to establish a permanent location. Key members of the curling fraternity (Noel Buxton, Bob Picken, Dorothy MacRae, to name but a few) accepted the challenge of trying to find a permanent site, building a plan that would turn a curling Hall of Fame from reality into fact. There was talk of a building in Assiniboine Park, Winnipeg, and a five-year lease was signed. But that plan fell through due to lack of funds.

Through the efforts of the 1986 Brier chairman, the late Mike Wagner of Kitchener, at the time a city councillor, a heritage building was obtained in Kitchener-Waterloo for a dollar a year, and a curator was hired. But a CCA fundraising project failed, and the dream died. Or if it didn't die, it had to be put on life support, which is still its current status.

More recently, the Saskatchewan Sports Hall of Fame and Museum, in Regina, offered space to the CCA for a National Curling Hall of Fame and Museum. While there is still hope that something concrete might materialize from discussions with the national body, so far the idea remains only a glimmer in the eyes of curlers in that hotbed of curling.

Some thirty or more years after the idea was first mooted, there is still no building in sight, and all the priceless pins, photos, and memorabilia that have been collected are stored in boxes somewhere in Ottawa. Each year a travelling Hall of Fame exhibit is available for viewing at either, or both, the Brier and the Hearts.

**A sometime experience of world curling fans is the robust singing—and toasting—to Scotland, the home of the game.**

*Photo by Michael Burns.*

### The Turner Curling Museum

There is however, another curling museum, albeit a private one, that is in existence in Weyburn, Saskatchewan, an hour or so down the road from Regina. A local curling enthusiast and perennial volunteer in the organization and operation of provincial, national and international curling events, Don Turner started out as a collector of curling pins. His collection soon expanded to include other items of curling memorabilia, and before long had outgrown the basement in the city home of Don and his wife Elva. Eventually, the city of Weyburn, attracted by the Turner's ever-expanding collection, offered space in a city building, and it has become a "must-see" stop for curlers everywhere.

## The Awards

Over the years, a variety of awards have been instituted at the various national and world championships. While some have names of important curlers (or builders of the game) attached to them, they mainly fit into two or three basic categories. And, as in most matters curling, the awards take their cue from the Brier.

An early trustee of the Brier was Ross Harstone of Hamilton, a small man in stature but with a booming voice, whose memory is kept alive through the Ross Harstone Award. It is given to the curler who, in its simplest terms, is the Most Sportsmanlike Curler at the Brier. The decision, avidly awaited each year, is made by a vote of the competing curlers.

In similar fashion, the Marj Mitchell Award honours the memory of the Regina skip who won Canada's first world title in 1980, only to succumb to cancer three years later at the age of 35. The award, given to the curler at the Scott Tournament of Hearts "who best embodies the spirit of curling," is decided by a vote of her peers.

It didn't take curling long to recognize the memory of Sandra Schmirler, the three-time Canadian and World winner who also skipped Canada's first Olympic gold medal team in 1998. Like Mitchell, Schmirler was a Regina curler, taken untimely from the world, at age 36. The Sandra Schmirler Award is given annually to the Most Valuable Player at the Hearts, as decided by a vote of the media present.

The Ray Kingsmith Executive-of-the-Year Award and the Joan Mead Award are similar honours. The former, which remembers a former Southern Alberta Curling Association secretary, who was also a long-time media personality, a popular CCA president, and chair of the curling at the 1988 Calgary Winter Olympics, is decided by the CCA. The national body, along with executives at Scott Paper, has a voice in selecting a builder of the game to receive the newly minted, in 2001, Joan Mead Award. Joan Mead was a long-time producer of CBC Curling events and a passionate advocate of the game, who died in 2000.

**Keith Wendorf has done it all. As the Canadian-born manager of the Rhine Valley CC at the Canadian Forces Base in Lahr, he had sufficient residency to skip the German national team on seven occasions, winning a silver medal in 1983. He has been a world-event official, team coach, and German national coach before becoming a development officer of the World Curling Federation. He is a two-time winner of the Colin A. Campbell Memorial Award and is also a winner of the World Curling Freytag Award.**

*Photo by Michael Burns.*

The CCA has also, in recent years, instituted a Volunteer of the Year Award, to honour a club volunteer who has performed valiantly at the local level. And the other Canadian events (Mixed, Seniors, and Juniors) also select winners of their sportsmanship awards.

At the world level, there are three awards, each with the name of a prominent curler attached. The Colin A. Campbell Memorial Award honours a world player at the Men's Championship, who, in the same fashion as the Harstone Award, is selected by a vote of his peers. The Frances Brodie Award, named after one of the leaders, from Scotland, and first chair, of the World Women's Championship, is also decided by a vote of the players. The Elmer Freytag Memorial Award honours the memory of the US curling executive, and lawyer,

**Bob Picken of Winnipeg, long-time curling reporter and former Canadian representative on the International Curling Federation, was honoured in Vancouver as the 1987 recipient of the Elmer Freytag Memorial Award.**
*Photo by Michael Burns.*

who was instrumental in elevating the ICF (later the WCF) from a committee of the RCCC into the independent international body that it is now. The award is given annually to someone who has helped promote international curling. Originally decided by a five-member media committee from around the world, it is now decided by a committee of the WCF.

\* \* \*

At one level there appears to be little in common between the curling that came to Canada in 1759 and today's game. Then it was irons; now it is granites. Then it was outdoors on natural ice; now it is indoors on artificial ice. Luck played a major role, skill a lesser role in the final result then; skill is the major component of victory now, though luck is still a factor. It would appear to be two different games, then and now. But look again and it's obvious that the game that started in a small way in a new land bears a striking resemblance to the game that captivates so many Canadians today. It's a game that beckons to Canadians of all ages and stages, in every province and territory. It was a slippery game then, and is so now. Laughter and camaraderie abound.

As William Weems put it so many years ago, "There's no game like curling. It's an honest sensible game. It's an honest couthie game is curling."

To which each of us who love curling say "amen."

# CHAPTER 17

# A Time Line of Curling

## In Scotland

1511    Date carved on Stirling stone, earliest indication of the beginning of curling.

1541    Challenge issued to "a tournament on ice," between John Slater and Gavin Hamilton—first written indication of the game (and probably a more civilized dispute mechanism than a duel).

1620    First known appearance of the word "curling" on a printed page.

1837    Victoria ascends throne of Great Britain.

1838    Formation of Grand Caledonian Curling Club (GCCC) in Scotland.

1842    Earl of Mansfield, as president of GCCC, entertains Queen Victoria and Prince Albert, and demonstrates curling on polished hardwood floor in the Long Hall of Scone Palace. He also presents Prince Albert with a pair of Ailsa Craig stones, with silver handles, and invites him to become first patron of the GCCC.

1843    Queen Victoria gives permission to have name of GCCC changed to Royal Caledonian Curling Club. Eventually, RCCC becomes the "Mother Club" of curling throughout the world.

1901    Victorian Era ends with death of Queen Victoria after reign of 64 years.


## In Canada

1760    Soldiers of the 78th Fraser Highlanders, serving under General Murray at the Battle of Ste. Foy in Quebec, create iron curling stones.

1807    Montreal Curling Club formed, with limited membership of 20. It becomes first sporting club in all North America.

1815    Napoleon defeated at Waterloo.

1819    Scots soldiers of Royal Staff Corps ask permission to melt down old cannonballs to make curling "irons." Blacksmith James Woods prepares mold, and sells cast iron stones for $3 each.

1820    First curling club in Ontario formed, in Kingston.

1820    Quebec City CC formed (membership reserved "for Scots only").

1824    First curling club in Nova Scotia formed in Halifax, due mainly to efforts of three gentlemen: Captain (later Admiral) Sir Houston Stewart, Colonel Greag and Dr. Grigor.

1828    Earl of Dalhousie listed as member of Quebec City CC.

1829    Coal discovered in New Glasgow (NS) and Scots miners, who have been brought to Canada, bring their curling stones with them.

1831    First curling club in US formed, at Orchard Lake (Detroit).

1834    Fergus CC (Ontario) formed.

1837    Unsuccessful rebellions in Upper and Lower Canada.
        Toronto CC formed.

        First covered curling rink built by Montreal CC in suburb of St. Anne, near Lachine Canal.

| 1839 | Curling stones advertised for sale, in Toronto, by Peter MacArthur, for $8 a pair. |
| 1844 | Act of Union joins Lower and Upper Canada. From 1845 to 1860, Canada has 12 different Federal governments. |
| 1845 | First curling club formed in Newfoundland (Avalon). |
| 1849 | California Gold Rush. |
| 1850 | Canada's population is less than three and a half million: most are under 45. |
| 1851 | All day, open-air match outside Truro between three teams from Halifax and three from Pictou (five players a side) draws 2,000 spectators. |
| 1852 | Formation of Canadian Branch, RCCC, in Montreal. |
| 1853 | Fredericton curling starts on frozen waters of Saint John River, followed shortly after by formation of clubs in Moncton, Saint John, and Newcastle. |
| 1858 | First Grand Match "East vs West" held in Toronto. |
| | Canadian Branch RCCC (in Montreal) issues invitation to Scots to tour Canada. Invitation accepted, but departure delayed for 44 years! |
| 1859 | First bonspiel on Toronto Bay. |
| 1860 | Potato Famine in Ireland, hard times in Britain send waves of immigrants to Canada. |
| | Toronto CC builds first covered rink in Ontario. |
| 1861 | Abraham Lincoln elected President of US. Four-year Civil War begins. |
| 1865 | First International curling Match, Canada vs USA, held at Buffalo, with 23 teams from each country participating. Canada wins 658–478. |
| | Abraham Lincoln assassinated. |

| 1867 | British North America Act establishes Dominion of Canada. |
| | John A. Macdonald becomes first Prime Minister. |
| 1874 | Ontario curlers split from Canadian Branch, RCCC (in Montreal) and form Ontario Branch, RCCC. Main reason is inability of Toronto/ Ontario curlers to get to Montreal for meetings, plus difference of opinion over best kind of curling stones: irons or granites. |
| 1875 | Toronto Granite Club formed. Sir John A. Macdonald listed as a member. |
| 1876 | First curling club in Manitoba (formed in Winnipeg). First match (using irons) held December 11. Losers donate a barrel of oatmeal to the hospital. |
| | Alexander Graham Bell invents telephone. |
| 1879 | Winnipeg game between City Fathers and Ordinary People, is won by latter. Aldermen have to pay forfeit of an oyster dinner. |
| 1880 | First curling in Saskatchewan (Prince Albert, Rosthern, and Battleford). |
| | Lord Dufferin institutes Governor General's prize for curling. |
| 1883 | First Montreal Winter Carnival held, and includes curling, sleigh races, horse races, tobogganing, and snowshoe races. |
| 1884 | First competition for the Gordon International Medal (Canada vs Grand National Curling Club) is played in Montreal, Brookline, and Utica. |
| 1885 | Curling started in Calgary. |
| | Canadian Pacific Railway completed. |
| 1886 | NB Branch of RCCC formed, but dies in 1891 ("lack of interest" cited). |

| | |
|---|---|
| 1887 | First curling club formed in PEI (Charlottetown). |
| 1888 | Manitoba Branch of RCCC formed with seven clubs (two in Winnipeg) as initial members. |
| | Calgary Curling Club affiliates with Manitoba Branch, RCCC. |
| 1889 | First Manitoba Bonspiel attracts 62 teams for three days of competition. |
| | First curling club formed in Regina. |
| | Number of ends, for important match, reduced from 24 to 20. |
| 1894 | First women's curling club organized in Montreal. |
| 1895 | First curling club formed in B.C. (Kaslo). |
| 1896 | Gold found at Bonanza Creek starts gold rush in Yukon. |
| 1898 | Kootenay Curling Association organizes bonspiel involving 18 rinks from Kaslo, Rossland, Sandon, and Revelstoke. |
| 1901 | Women's curling clubs spring up in Lachine, Ottawa, Arnprior, Toronto, Kingston, and Revelstoke. |
| 1902 | December 26, 28 Scots curlers arrive in Halifax for first Scots tour of Canada. The visit covers a total of 9,918 miles [16 000 km] over two months. The visitors depart New York City February 18, 1903 (further details in chapter 6). |
| 1903 | Major, later Colonel, Walker, North West Mounted Police, suggests formation of Western Curling Association, separate from the Manitoba and Northwest Territories Branch, RCCC. The attempt is defeated. |
| 1904 | Major Walker tries again and this time is successful: Alberta Branch, RCCC formed. |
| 1906 | B.C. Branch, RCCC, formed. |

| | |
|---|---|
| 1907 | Alberta wins first interprovincial match with Saskatchewan. |
| 1908 | Manitoba Branch, RCCC, becomes Manitoba Curling Association. |
| 1909 | First Canadian touring team travels to Scotland and wins 23 of 26 matches. |
| 1910 | Five-day work week begun in the US: the "weekend" becomes instituted. |
| 1911 | Second touring Scottish team comes to Canada. Scots are beaten in four Strathcona Cup matches held in Maritimes, Quebec, Ontario, and Manitoba. |
| 1912 | SS *Titanic* sinks: 1,513 drown. |
| 1913 | Ladies' events added to Manitoba Bonspiel. Ontario Curling Association inaugurates Ladies' Tankard, won by Belleville team. |
| 1918 | Ninety-one rinks enter Alberta Curling Association bonspiel, making it the "biggest ever held west of Winnipeg." |
| | Federal Minister of Health bans all sporting events from mid-October to early November to combat Spanish flu epidemic. |
| 1921 | Canadian proposal to International Olympic Committee accepted; proposal states that future host cities could include a sport of their choice. |
| 1922 | Insulin isolated by Frederick Banting and Charles Best. |
| 1924 | First Olympic Winter Festival held in Chamonix, France, with three countries (Sweden, Great Britain, and France) participating in curling competition. GBR wins gold. |
| 1925 | IOC, retroactively, accepts 1924 Olympic Winter Festival as first official Olympic Winter Games. |

| 1927 | First Macdonald Brier held at Granite Club in Toronto. Game length is 14 ends. |
| | Charles Lindbergh flies across Atlantic. First talking motion picture, *The Jazz Singer*, stars Al Jolson. |
| 1928 | Brier reduces length of game from 14 ends to 12. |
| 1929 | British Privy Council overturns Canada's Supreme Court and rules women are "persons." |
| 1932 | Eight teams entered in Lake Placid Winter Olympics III, four from USA and four from Canada. Winnipeg team wins gold. |
| 1934 | PEI Curling Association formed. |
| 1935 | Dominion Curling Association formed in meetings at Toronto Granite Club. |
| 1940 | First Brier held outside Toronto, at the Amphitheatre in Winnipeg. |
| 1943–45 | Brier play suspended during World War II. |
| 1945 | Harold Covell, principal at Regina's Lakeview School, introduces jam-can curling for younger children. |
| 1947 | First carspiel held in Nipawin, Saskatchewan. Four Hudson sedans, valued at $2,200 each, put up as prizes. Over 500 curlers are attracted to the event, won by Howard "Pappy" Wood. |
| 1949 | Ken Watson of Winnipeg becomes first skip to win three Brier titles. |
| 1950 | Watson helps inaugurate Canadian School Curling Championship. First event is held in Quebec City. |
| 1959 | First Scotch Cup matches held in Scotland. Ernie Richardson (Canada) plays Willie Young (Scotland) and wins. Invitational event is forerunner to World Curling Championship. |

| 1960 | Unique East–West women's playoff, in Oshawa, won by Joyce McKee rink from Saskatchewan. Canadian Ladies' Curling Association is founded, and Dominion Stores accepted as sponsor of CLCA Championship. |
|------|------|
| 1961 | Dominion Diamond D Ladies' Championship held in Ottawa, with teams from every province represented. Joyce McKee rink (Saskatchewan) is winner. |
| 1964 | First Canadian Mixed Championship (sponsored by O'Keefe Breweries) held in Toronto. Ernie Boushy rink (Manitoba) is winner. |
| | Beatles make first North American trip and Beatlemania sweeps North America. |
| 1965 | First Canadian Senior Men's Championship (over 55) held in Ft. William. Winner is Leo Johnson of Manitoba. |
| 1966 | International Curling Federation established as committee of RCCC during Scotch Cup matches in Calgary. |
| 1967 | Last Dominion Diamond D Championship held in Town of Mt. Royal, Montreal. Winner is Betty Duguid rink from Manitoba. CLCA takes over running of event. |
| 1968 | First CLCA championship held in Winnipeg (St. James Civic Centre). Title won by Hazel Jamieson team (Alberta). |
| | First Air Canada Silver Broom held in Pointe Claire (Quebec). Canada's Ron Northcott is winner. Two teams set Guinness Book of Records mark for endurance by playing 26 hours, 15 minutes in Yellowknife, NWT. |
| 1969 | Neil Armstrong becomes first man on the moon. |
| 1971 | Canadian Junior Women's Championship inaugurated in Vancouver. Only four western teams compete. Winner is Shelby MacKenzie of Alberta. |

| 1972 | Macdonald Tobacco becomes sponsor of CLCA Championship. First "Lassie" is held in Saskatoon. Vera Pezer team (Saskatchewan) is winner. |
|------|------|
| 1973 | First Canadian Senior Ladies' Championship held in Ottawa. Winner is Ada Calles of British Columbia. |
| | Brier officials agree a team may concede victory to opponent. |
| 1975 | Brier expanded to 12 teams with inclusion of team from Yukon/NWT. |
| 1977 | Brier reduces length of game from 12 ends to 10. |
| 1978 | New endurance record set when two B.C. rinks play 61 hours, 20 minutes. |
| 1979 | Last Lassie Championship held in Town of Mt. Royal, Montreal. Lindsay Sparkes (BC) is winner. |
| | First Ladies' World Curling Championship held in Perth, Scotland. Winner is Gaby Casanova of Switzerland. |
| 1980 | CLCA assumes management of Canadian Ladies' Championship, and continues for two years. |
| | NB Men's and Ladies' curling associations first to amalgamate in Canada. |
| 1982 | First Scott Tournament of Hearts held in Regina. Winner is Colleen Jones of Nova Scotia. |
| | Guinness Book of Records shows marathon curling record set when eight junior curlers at the Capital Winter Club in Fredericton play for 73 hrs, 54 minutes. |
| 1985 | Final Air Canada Silver Broom held in Glasgow. Winner is Al Hackner of Canada. |

| 1986 | Hexagon International becomes sponsor of World Curling Championship, held in Toronto. First winner is Ed Lukowich of Canada. |
|---|---|
| 1988 | Calgary hosts Winter Olympics, where curling is a demonstration event. |
| | Linda Moore wins gold for Canada in women's event; Eigil Ramsfjell wins gold for Norway in men's event. Ed Lukowich wins bronze. |
| | Final Hexagon WCC held in Lausanne. Winner is Eigil Ramsfjell. |
| 1989 | World Men's and Women's Championships combined into single event in Milwaukee. Time clocks introduced to world play. |
| 1991 | Moncton 100 Bonspiel introduces the Howard Rule, which is modified later to become Free Guard Zone rule. |
| | ICF changes name to World Curling Federation in order to avoid confusion with canoeing. |
| 1992 | Curling, a demonstration sport at Albertville Winter Olympics, is held in Pralognan la Vanoise, and modified version of Howard Rule is introduced under name of Free Guard Zone rule. Urs Dick (Switzerland) wins gold in men's event. Andrea Schöpp (Germany) wins gold in women's event. Julie Sutton (Canada) wins bronze. |
| | In July, IOC confirms curling as a medal sport for 2002 Winter Games, but indicates it could be negotiable as a medal sport in 1998. Nagano negotiates to have curling accepted as part of its 1998 Winter Olympics. |
| | World Curling Tour inaugurated, and World Curling Players' Association formed (with Ed Lukowich as president). |
| 1995 | Ford of Canada assumes sponsorship of World Curling Championships. First Ford Worlds held in Brandon. Kerry Burtnyk (Canada) wins men's title. Elisabet Gustafson (Sweden) wins women's. |

| 1998 | First Winter Olympics with curling as a full-fledged medal sport. Sandra Schmirler wins gold medal for Canada in women's event. Patrick Hurlimann wins gold medal for Switzerland in men's event. Mike Harris (Canada) wins silver. |
| --- | --- |
| 2001 | Grand Slam of Curling begun with $100,000 cashspiels in Wainwright, AB; Gander, NF; and Sault Ste. Marie, ON. Grand Slam completed with World Curling Tour Players' Championship in Strathroy, ON. |
| 2002 | XIX Winter Olympic Games held in Ogden, Utah. Pål Trulsen (Norway) wins gold in men's event. Rhona Martin (Great Britain) wins gold in women's event. Canadian men (Kevin Martin) win silver medal. Canadian women (Kelley Law) win bronze. |
| | WCF accepts wheelchair curling as an official sport. First World Wheelchair Curling Championship held in Sursee, Switzerland. Canada wins silver. |
| | WCF accepts World Seniors competition (men and women) as an official event. First World Seniors Championships held in Bismark (US) at same time as Ford Worlds event. USA (Larry Johnston) wins men's event. Canada (Anne Dunn) wins women's event. |
| | Continental Cup international curling series (North America vs Rest of World) begun in Regina, with six teams each side playing variety of events. |
| 2003 | Scotland sends touring teams to Canada one hundred years after first visit by Scots. |
| | Canada Cup of Curling begun in Kamloops, BC. |

# CHAPTER 18

# Roster of Royalty

**If there is a roster of royalty in Canadian curling, it surely is the roll call of** champions in a variety of national and international championships.

There are some members of the media who have memories for names, times, and places that are just as accurate as the memories some national champions have for significant shots and special occasions in their illustrious careers. For the most part, however, media rely on the data banks of national or world curling associations for significant names and dates. Occasionally, and usually late at night from some sports bar, a member of the media will receive a phone call asking for a specific bit of information about one or more famous curling names. "To settle an argument we're having," is the usual phrase that accompanies the request.

In order to diminish the number of such future requests, here are the lists of the various Canadian (and World) championship teams, with a note of appreciation to the Canadian Curling Association and Laurie Payne of the St. Clair Group for the provision of the details.

## The Canadian Men's Champions

| 2002 | Alberta | Randy Ferbey, David Nedohin, Scott Pfeifer, Marcel Rocque |
| 2001 | Alberta | Randy Ferbey, David Nedohin, Scott Pfeifer, Marcel Rocque |
| 2000 | British Columbia | Greg McAulay, Brent Pierce, Bryan Miki, Jody Sveistrup |
| 1999 | Manitoba | Jeff Stoughton, Jonathan Mead, Garry Vandenberghe, Doug Armstrong |
| 1998 | Ontario | Wayne Middaugh, Graeme McCarrel, Ian Tetley, Scott Bailey |
| 1997 | Alberta | Kevin Martin, Don Walchuk, Rudy Ramcharan, Don Bartlett |
| 1996 | Manitoba | Jeff Stoughton, Ken Tresoor, Garry Vandenberghe, Steve Gould |
| 1995 | Manitoba | Kerry Burtnyk, Jeff Ryan, Rob Meakin, Keith Fenton |
| 1994 | British Columbia | Rick Folk, Pat Ryan, Bert Gretzinger, Gerry Richard |
| 1993 | Ontario | Russ Howard, Glenn Howard, Wayne Middaugh, Peter Corner |
| 1992 | Manitoba | Vic Peters, Dan Carey, Chris Neufeld, Don Rudd |
| 1991 | Alberta | Kevin Martin, Kevin Park, Dan Petryk, Don Bartlett |
| 1990 | Ontario | Ed Werenich, John Kawaja, Ian Tetley, Pat Perroud |
| 1989 | Alberta | Pat Ryan, Randy Ferbey, Don Walchuk, Don McKenzie |
| 1988 | Alberta | Pat Ryan, Randy Ferbey, Don Walchuk, Don McKenzie |
| 1987 | Ontario | Russ Howard, Glenn Howard, Tim Belcourt, Kent Carstairs |
| 1986 | Alberta | Ed Lukowich, John Ferguson, Neil Houston, Brent Syme |
| 1985 | Northern Ontario | Al Hackner, Rick Lang, Ian Tetley, Pat Perroud |
| 1984 | Manitoba | Mike Riley, Brian Toews, John Helston, Russ Wookey |
| 1983 | Ontario | Ed Werenich, Paul Savage, John Kawaja, Neil Harrison |
| 1982 | Northern Ontario | Al Hackner, Rick Lang, Bob Nicol, Bruce Kennedy |
| 1981 | Manitoba | Kerry Burtynk, Mark Olson, Jim Spencer, Ron Kammerlock |
| 1980 | Saskatchewan | Rick Folk, Ron Mills, Tom Wilson, Jim Wilson |
| 1979 | Manitoba | Barry Fry, Bill Carey, Gord Sparkes, Bryan Wood |
| 1978 | Alberta | Ed Lukowich, Mike Chernoff, Dale Johnston, Ron Schindle |
| 1977 | Quebec | Jim Ursel, Art Lobel, Don Aitken, Brian Ross |
| 1976 | Newfoundland | Jack MacDuff, Toby McDonald, Doug Hudson, Ken Templeton |

| 1975 | Northern Ontario | Bill Tetley, Rick Lang, Bill Hodgson, Peter Hnatiw |
|------|------------------|---------------------------------------------------|
| 1974 | Alberta | Hec Gervais, Ron Anton, Warren Hansen, Darrel Sutton |
| 1973 | Saskatchewan | Harvey Mazinke, Billy Martin, George Achtymichuk, Dan Klippenstein |
| 1972 | Manitoba | Orest Meleschuk, Dave Romano, John Hanesiak, Pat Hailley |
| 1971 | Manitoba | Don Duguid, Rod Hunter, Jim Pettapiece, Bryan Wood |
| 1970 | Manitoba | Don Duguid, Rod Hunter, Jim Pettapiece, Bryan Wood |
| 1969 | Alberta | Ron Northcott, Dave Gerlach, Bernie Sparkes, Fred Storey |
| 1968 | Alberta | Ron Northcott, Jim Shields, Bernie Sparkes, Fred Storey |
| 1967 | Ontario | Alf Phillips Jr., John Ross, Ron Manning, Keith Reilly |
| 1966 | Alberta | Ron Northcott, George Fink, Bernie Sparkes, Fred Storey |
| 1965 | Manitoba | Terry Braunstein, Don Duguid, Ron Braunstein, Ray Turnbull |
| 1964 | British Columbia | Lyall Dagg, Leo Hebert, Fred Britton, Barry Naimark |
| 1963 | Saskatchewan | Ernie Richardson, Arnold Richardson, Garnet Richardson, Mel Perry |
| 1962 | Saskatchewan | Ernie Richardson, Arnold Richardson, Garnet Richardson, Wes Richardson |
| 1961 | Alberta | Hec Gervais, Ron Anton, Ray Werner, Wally Ursuliak |
| 1960 | Saskatchewan | Ernie Richardson, Arnold Richardson, Garnet Richardson, Wes Richardson |
| 1959 | Saskatchewan | Ernie Richardson, Arnold Richardson, Garnet Richardson, Wes Richardson |
| 1958 | Alberta | Matt Baldwin, Jack Geddes, Gordon Haynes, Bill Price |
| 1957 | Alberta | Matt Baldwin, Gordon Haynes, Art Kleinmeyer, Bill Price |
| 1956 | Manitoba | Billy Walsh, Al Langlois, Cy White, Andy McWilliams |
| 1955 | Saskatchewan | Garnet Campbell, Don Campbell, Glenn Campbell, Lloyd Campbell |
| 1954 | Alberta | Matt Baldwin, Glenn Gray, Pete Ferry, Jim Collins |
| 1953 | Manitoba | Ab Gowanlock, Jim Williams, Art Pollon, Russ Jackman |
| 1952 | Manitoba | Billy Walsh, Al Langlois, Andy McWilliams, John Watson |
| 1951 | Nova Scotia | Don Oyler, George Hanson, Fred Dyke, Wally Knock |
| 1950 | Northern Ontario | Tom Ramsay, Len Williamson, Bill Weston, Bill Kenny |

| 1949 | Manitoba | Ken Watson, Grant Watson, Lyle Dyker, Charles Read |
| 1948 | British Columbia | Frenchy D'Amour, Bob McGhie, Fred Wendell, Jim Mark |
| 1947 | Manitoba | Jimmy Welsh, Alex Welsh, Jack Reid, Harry Monk |
| 1946 | Alberta | Bill Rose, Bart Swelin, Austin Smith, George Crooks |
| 1942 | Manitoba | Ken Watson, Grant Watson, Charlie Scrymgeour, Jim Grant |
| 1941 | Alberta | Howard Palmer, Jack Lebeau, Art Gooder, Clare Webb |
| 1940 | Manitoba | Howard Wood, Ernie Pollard, Howard Wood Jr., Roy Enman |
| 1939 | Ontario | Bert Hall, Perry Hall, Ernie Parkes, Cam Seagram |
| 1938 | Manitoba | Ab Gowanlock, Bung Cartmell, Bill McKnight, Tom McKnight |
| 1937 | Alberta | Cliff Manahan, Wes Robinson, Ross Manahan, Lloyd McIntyre |
| 1936 | Manitoba | Ken Watson, Grant Watson, Marvin McIntyre, Charles Kerr |
| 1935 | Ontario | Gordon Campbell, Don Campbell, Gord Coates, Duncan Campbell |
| 1934 | Manitoba | Leo Johnson, Lorne Stewart, Linc Johnson, Marno Frederickson |
| 1933 | Alberta | Cliff Manahan, Harold Deeton, Harold Wolfe, Bert Ross |
| 1932 | Manitoba | Jimmy Congalton, Howard Wood, Bill Noble, Harry Mawhinney |
| 1931 | Manitoba | Bob Gourlay, Ernie Pollard, Arnold Lockerbie, Ray Stewart |
| 1930 | Manitoba | Howard Wood, Jimmy Congalton, Victor Wood, Lionel Wood |
| 1929 | Manitoba | Gordon Hudson, Don Rollo, Ron Singbusch, Bill Grant |
| 1928 | Manitoba | Gordon Hudson, Sam Penwarden, Ron Singbusch, Bill Grant |
| 1927 | Nova Scotia | Murray Macneill, Al MacInnes, Cliff Torey, Jim Donahoe |

## The Canadian Women's Champions

| 2002 | Team Canada | Colleen Jones, Kim Kelly, Mary-Anne Waye, Nancy Delahunt |
| 2001 | Nova Scotia | Colleen Jones, Kim Kelly, Mary-Anne Waye, Nancy Delahunt |

| 2000 | British Columbia | Kelley Law, Julie Skinner, Georgina Wheatcroft, Diane Nelson |
| 1999 | Nova Scotia | Colleen Jones, Kim Kelly, Mary-Anne Waye, Nancy Delahunt |
| 1998 | Alberta | Cathy Borst, Heather Godberson, Brenda Bohmer, Kate Horne |
| 1997 | Saskatchewan | Sandra Schmirler, Jan Betker, Joan McCusker, Marcia Gudereit |
| 1996 | Ontario | Marilyn Bodogh, Kim Gellard, Corie Beveridge, Jane Hooper Perroud |
| 1995 | Manitoba | Connie Laliberte, Cathy Overton, Cathy Gauthier, Janet Arnott |
| 1994 | Team Canada | Sandra Peterson, Jan Betker, Joan McCusker, Marcia Gudereit |
| 1993 | Saskatchewan | Sandra Peterson, Jan Betker, Joan McCusker, Marcia Gudereit |
| 1992 | Manitoba | Connie Laliberte, Laurie Allen, Cathy Gauthier, Janet Arnott |
| 1991 | British Columbia | Julie Sutton, Jodie Sutton, Melissa Soligo, Karri Willms |
| 1990 | Ontario | Alison Goring, Kristin Turcotte, Andrea Lawes, Cheryl McPherson |
| 1989 | Team Canada | Heather Houston, Lorraine Lang, Diane Adams, Tracy Kennedy |
| 1988 | Ontario | Heather Houston, Lorraine Lang, Diane Adams, Tracy Kennedy |
| 1987 | British Columbia | Pat Sanders, Georgina Hawkes, Louise Herlinveaux, Deb Massullo |
| 1986 | Ontario | Marilyn Darte, Kathy McEdwards, Chris Jurgenson, Jan Augustyn |
| 1985 | British Columbia | Linda Moore, Lindsay Sparkes, Debbie Jones, Laurie Carney |
| 1984 | Manitoba | Connie Laliberte, Chris More, Corinne Peters, Janet Arnott |
| 1983 | Nova Scotia | Penny LaRocque, Sharon Horne, Cathy Caudle, Pam Sanford |
| 1982 | Nova Scotia | Colleen Jones, Kay Smith, Monica Jones, Barbara Jones-Gordon |
| 1981 | Alberta | Susan Seitz, Judy Erickson, Myrna McKay, Betty McCracken |
| 1980 | Saskatchewan | Marj Mitchell, Nancy Kerr, Shirley McKendry, Wendy Leach |

| 1979 | British Columbia | Lindsay Sparkes, Dawn Knowles, Robin Wilson, Lorraine Bowles |
| 1978 | Manitoba | Cathy Pidzarko, Chris Pidzarko, Iris Armstrong, Patty Vanderkerckhove |
| 1977 | Alberta | Myrna McQuarrie, Rita Tarnava, Barb Davis, Jane Rempel |
| 1976 | British Columbia | Lindsay Davie, Dawn Knowles, Robin Klassen, Lorraine Bowles |
| 1975 | Quebec | Lee Tobin, Marilyn McNeil, Michelle Garneau, Laurie Ross |
| 1974 | Saskatchewan | Emily Farnham, Linda Saunders, Pat McBeath, Donna Collins |
| 1973 | Saskatchewan | Vera Pezer, Sheila Rowan, Joyce McKee, Lenore Morrison |
| 1972 | Saskatchewan | Vera Pezer, Sheila Rowan, Joyce McKee, Lenore Morrison |
| 1971 | Saskatchewan | Vera Pezer, Sheila Rowan, Joyce McKee, Lenore Morrison |
| 1970 | Saskatchewan | Dorenda Schoenhals, Cheryl Stirton, Linda Burnham, Joan Anderson |
| 1969 | Saskatchewan | Joyce McKee, Vera Pezer, Lenore Morrison, Jennifer Falk |
| 1968 | Alberta | Hazel Jamieson, Gail Lee, Jackie Spencer, June Coyle |
| 1967 | Manitoba | Betty Duguid, Joan Ingram, Laurie Bradawaski, Dot Rose |
| 1966 | Alberta | Gail Lee, Hazel Jamieson, Sharon Harrington, June Coyle |
| 1965 | Manitoba | Peggy Casselman, Val Taylor, Pat MacDonald, Pat Scott |
| 1964 | British Columbia | Ina Hansen, Ada Callas, Isabel Leith, May Shaw |
| 1963 | New Brunswick | Mabel DeWare, Harriet Stratton, Forbis Stevenson, Marjorie Fraser |
| 1962 | British Columbia | Ina Hansen, Ada Callas, Isabel Leith, May Shaw |
| 1961 | Saskatchewan | Joyce McKee, Sylvia Fedoruk, Barbara MacNevin, Rosa McFee |
| 1960 | Saskatchewan | Joyce McKee, Sylvia Fedoruk, Donna Belding, Muriel Coben |

## The Canadian Junior Men's Champions

| 2002 | Manitoba | David Hamblin, Ross Derksen, Kevin Hamblin, Ross McCannell |
| 2001 | Newfoundland | Brad Gushue, Mark Nichols, Brent Hamilton, Mike Adam |
| 2000 | British Columbia | Brad Kuhn, Kevin Folk, Ryan Kuhn, Hugh Bennett |

| 1999 | Ontario | John Morris, Craig Savill, Jason Young, Brent Laing |
| 1998 | Ontario | John Morris, Craig Savill, Andy Ormsby, Brent Laing |
| 1997 | Alberta | Ryan Keane, Scott Pfeifer, Blayne Iskiw, Peter Heck |
| 1996 | Northern Ontario | Jeff Currie, Greg Given, Andrew Mikkelsen, Tyler Oinonen |
| 1995 | Manitoba | Chris Galbraith, Scott Cripps, Brent Barrett, Bryan Galbraith |
| 1994 | Alberta | Colin Davison, Kelly Mittelstadt, Scott Pfeifer, Sean Morris |
| 1993 | Nova Scotia | Shawn Adams, Ben Blanchard, Jon Philip, Robert MacArthur |
| 1992 | Quebec | Michel Ferland, Marco Berthelot, Steve Beaudry, Steve Guetre |
| 1991 | Northern Ontario | Jason Repay, Aaron Skillen, Scott McCallum, Trevor Clifford |
| 1990 | Ontario | Noel Herron, Robert Brewer, Steve Small, Richard Polk |
| 1989 | British Columbia | Dean Joanisse, David Nantes, Tim Coomes, Jef Pilon |
| 1988 | British Columbia | Mike Wood, Mike Bradley, Todd Troyer, Greg Hawkes |
| 1987 | New Brunswick | Jim Sullivan, Charlie Sullivan, Craig Burgess, Dan Alderman |
| 1986 | Manitoba | Hugh McFadyen, Jon Mead, Norman Gould, John Lange |
| 1985 | Alberta | Kevin Martin, Richard Feeney, Daniel Petryk, Michael Berger |
| 1984 | Manitoba | Bob Ursel, Brent Mendella, Gerald Chick, Mike Ursel |
| 1983 | Saskatchewan | Jamie Schneider, Danny Ferner, Steven Leippi, Kelly Vollman |
| 1982 | Ontario | John Base, Bruce Webster, Dave McAnerney, Jim Donahoe |
| 1981 | Manitoba | Mert Thompsett, Bill McTavish, Joel Gagne, Mike Friesen |
| 1980 | Quebec | Denis Marchand, Denis Cecil, Yves Barrette, Larry Phillips |
| 1979 | Manitoba | Mert Thompsett, Lyle Derry, Joel Gagne, Mike Friesen |
| 1978 | Alberta | Darren Fish, Lorne Barker, Murray Ursulak, Barry Barker |
| 1977 | Alberta | Paul Gowsell, John Ferguson, Doug MacFarlane, Kelly Stearne |
| 1976 | P.E.I. | Bill Jenkins, John Scales, Sandy Stewart, Alan Mayhew |
| 1975 | Alberta | Paul Gowsell, Neil Houston, Glen Jackson, Kelly Stearne |
| 1974 | Alberta | Robb King, Brad Hannah, Bill Fowlis, Chris King |
| 1973 | Ontario | Mark McDonald, Lloyd Emmerson, Phillip Tomsett, Jon Clare |
| 1972 | Alberta | Lawrence Niven, Rick Niven, Jim Ross, Ted Poblawski |

| 1971 | Saskatchewan | Greg Montgomery, Don Despins, Jeff Montgomery, Rod Verboom |
| 1970 | New Brunswick | Ronald Ferguson, Garth Jardine, Brian Henderson, Cyril Sutherland |
| 1969 | Saskatchewan | Robert Miller, Roger Rask, Lloyd Helm, William Aug |
| 1968 | Ontario | William Hope, Bruce Lord, Brian Domney, Dennis Gardiner |
| 1967 | Alberta | Stanley Trout, Doug Dobry, Allan Kullay, Donald Douglas |
| 1966 | Alberta | Brian Howes, Blair Pallesen, John Thompson, Chris Robinson |
| 1965 | Saskatchewan | Dan Fink, Ken Runtz, Ron Jacques, Larry Lechner |
| 1964 | Northern Ontario | Bob Ash, Bill Ash, Gerry Armstrong, Fred Prier |
| 1963 | Alberta | Wayne Saboe, Ron Hampton, Rick Aldridge, Mick Adams |
| 1962 | Saskatchewan | Mike Lukowich, Ed Lukowich, Doug McLeod, David Moore |
| 1961 | British Columbia | Jerry Caughlin, Jack Cox, Mike Shippitt, David Jones |
| 1960 | Alberta | Tommy Kroeger, Jack Isaman, Ron Nelson, Murray Sorenson |
| 1959 | Alberta | John Trout, Bruce Walker, Dave Woods, Allen Sharpe |
| 1958 | Northern Ontario | Tom Tod, Neil McLeod, Patrick Moran, David Allin |
| 1957 | Ontario | Ian Johnston, Peter Galsworthy, Dave Robinson, Mike Jackson |
| 1956 | Saskatchewan | Bob Hawkins, Ted Clarke, Bruce Beveridge, Dave Williams |
| 1955 | Saskatchewan | Bayne Secord, Stan Austman, Merv Mann, Gary Stevenson |
| 1954 | Saskatchewan | Bayne Secord, Don Snider, Stan Austman, Don Brownell |
| 1953 | Ontario | Bob Walker, Duncan Brodie, Claire Peacock, George MacGregor |
| 1952 | Saskatchewan | Gary Thode, Gary Cooper, Doug Conn, Roy Hufsmith |
| 1951 | Saskatchewan | Gary Thode, Gary Cooper, Orest Hyrniuk, Roy Hufsmith |
| 1950 | Saskatchewan | Bill Clarke, Gary Carlson, Ian Innes, Harold Grassie |

## The Canadian Junior Women's Champions

| 2002 | P.E.I. | Suzanne Gaudet, Robyn MacPhee, Carol Webb, Kelly Higgins |
| 2001 | P.E.I. | Suzanne Gaudet, Stefanie Richard, Robyn MacPhee, Kelly Higgins |

| 2000 | Saskatchewan | Stefanie Miller, Marliese Miller, Stacy Helm, Amanda MacDonald |
| 1999 | Quebec | Marie-France Larouche, Nancy Bélanger, Marie-Eve Létourneau, Valerie Grenier |
| 1998 | New Brunswick | Melissa McClure, Nancy Toner, Brigitte McClure, Bethany Toner |
| 1997 | Nova Scotia | Meredith Doyle, Beth Roach, Tara Hamer, Candice MacLean |
| 1996 | Alberta | Heather Godberson, Carmen Whyte, Kristie Moore, Terelyn Bloor |
| 1995 | Manitoba | Kelly MacKenzie, Joanne Fillion, Carlene Muth, Sasha Bergner |
| 1994 | Manitoba | Jennifer Jones, Trisha Baldwin, Jill Officer, Dana Malanchuk |
| 1993 | Ontario | Kim Gellard, Corie Beveridge, Lisa Savage, Sandy Graham |
| 1992 | Saskatchewan | Amber Holland, Cindy Street, Tracy Beach, Angela Street |
| 1991 | New Brunswick | Heather Smith, Denis Cormier, Suzanne LeBlanc, Lesley Hicks |
| 1990 | Saskatchewan | Atina Ford, Darlene Kidd, Leslie Beck, Cindy Ford |
| 1989 | Manitoba | Cathy Overton, Tracy Baldwin, Carol Harvey, Tracy Bush |
| 1988 | Alberta | LeDawn Funk, Sandy Symyrozum, Cindy Larsen, Laurelle Funk |
| 1987 | British Columbia | Julie Sutton, Judy Wood, Susan Auty, Marla Geiger |
| 1986 | British Columbia | Jodie Sutton, Julie Sutton, Dawn Rubner, Chris Thompson |
| 1985 | Saskatchewan | Kimberley Armbruster, Sheila Calcutt, Wanda Figitt, Lorraine Krupski |
| 1984 | Manitoba | Darcy Kirkness, Barb Kirkness, Janet Harvey, Barbara Fetch |
| 1983 | Ontario | Alison Goring, Kristin Holman, Cheryl McPherson, Lynda Armstrong |
| 1982 | British Columbia | Sandra Plut, Sandra Rainey, Leigh Fraser, Debra Fowles |
| 1981 | Manitoba | Karen Fallis, Karen Tresoor, Caroline Hunter, Lynn Fallis |
| 1980 | Nova Scotia | Kay Smith, Krista Gatchell, Cathy Caudle, Peggy Wilson |
| 1979 | Saskatchewan | Denise Wilson, Judy Walker, Dianne Choquette, Shannon Olafson |
| 1978 | Alberta | Cathy King, Brenda Oko, Maureen Olsen, Diane Bowes |

| 1977 | Alberta | Cathy King, Robin Ursuliak, Maureen Olsen, Mary Kay James |
| 1976 | Saskatchewan | Colleen Rudd, Carol Rudd, Julie Burke, Lori Glenn |
| 1975 | Saskatchewan | Patricia Crimp, Colleen Rudd, Judy Sefton, Merrill Greabeiel |
| 1974 | Manitoba | Chris Pidzarko, Cathy Pidzarko, Patti Vanderkerckhove, Barbara Rudolph |
| 1973 | Saskatchewan | Janet Crimp, Carol Davis, Chris Gervais, Susan Carney |
| 1972 | Manitoba | Chris Pidzarko, Cathy Pidzarko, Beth Brunsden, Barbara Rudolph |
| 1971 | Alberta | Shelby McKenzie, Marlene Pargeter, Arlene Hrdlicka, Debbie Goliss |

## The Canadian Mixed Champions

| 2002 | Nova Scotia | Mark Dacey, Heather Smith-Dacey, Rob Harris, Laine Peters |
| 2001 | Quebec | Jean Michel Ménard, Jessica Marchand, Marco Berthelot, Joëlle Sabourin |
| 2000 | Alberta | Kevin Koe, Susan O'Connor, Greg Northcott, Lawnie Goodfellow |
| 1999 | Nova Scotia | Paul Flemming, Colleen Jones, Tom Fetterly, Monica Moriarty |
| 1998 | Nova Scotia | Steve Ogden, Mary Mattatall, Jeff Hopkins, Heather Hopkins |
| 1997 | Northern Ontario | Chris Johnson, Barb McKinty, Drew Eloranta, Lisa Gauvreau |
| 1996 | Saskatchewan | Randy Bryden, Cathy Trowell, Russ Bryden, Karen Inglis |
| 1995 | Nova Scotia | Steve Ogden, Mary Mattatall, Jeff Hopkins, Heather Hopkins |
| 1994 | New Brunswick | Grant Odishaw, Heather Smith, Rick Perron, Krista Smith |
| 1993 | Nova Scotia | Scott Saunders, Colleen Jones, Tom Fetterly, Helen Radford |
| 1992 | Alberta | Kurt Balderston, Marcy Balderston, Rod Kramer, Joanne Morrison |
| 1991 | Manitoba | Jeff Stoughton, Karen Fallis, Scott Morrow, Lynn Morrow |
| 1990 | Alberta | Marvin Wirth, Glenna Rubin, Millard Evans, Robin Pettit |
| 1989 | P.E.I. | Robert Campbell, Angela Roberts, Mark O'Rourke, Kathy O'Rourke |
| 1988 | Manitoba | Jeff Stoughton, Karen Fallis, Rob Meakin, Lynn Morrow |

| 1987 | P.E.I. | Peter Gallant, Kathy Gallant, Phil Gorveatte, Simone MacKenzie |
| 1986 | Ontario | Dave Van Dine, Dawn Ventura, Hugh Millikin, Cindy Wiggins |
| 1985 | British Columbia | Steve Skillings, Pat Sanders, Al Carlson, Louise Herlinveaux |
| 1984 | Saskatchewan | Randy Woytowich, Kathy Fahlman, Brian McCusker, Jan Betker |
| 1983 | Saskatchewan | Rick Folk, Dorenda Schoenhals, Tom Wilson, Elizabeth Folk |
| 1982 | British Columbia | Glen Pierce, Marlene Neubauer, Fuji Miki, Sharon Bradley |
| 1981 | Northern Ontario | Rick Lang, Anne Provo, Bert Provo, Lorraine Edwards |
| 1980 | Manitoba | Jim Dunstone, Carol Dunstone, Del Stitt, Elaine Jones |
| 1979 | Northern Ontario | Roy Lund, Nancy Lund, Ron Apland, Marsha Kerr |
| 1978 | Saskatchewan | Bernie Yuzdepski, Marnie McNiven, Roy Uchman, Joan Bjerke |
| 1977 | Manitoba | Harold Tanasichuk, Rose Tanasichuk, Jim Kirkness, Debbie Orr |
| 1976 | British Columbia | Tony Eberts, Elizabeth Short, Clark Glanville, Eleanor Short |
| 1975 | Alberta | Les Rowland, Audrey Rowland, Dan Schmaltz, Betty Schmaltz |
| 1974 | Saskatchewan | Rick Folk, Cheryl Stirton, Tom Wilson, Bonnie Orchard |
| 1973 | Manitoba | Barry Fry, Peggy Casselman, Stephen Decter, Susan Lynch |
| 1972 | British Columbia | Trev Fisher, Gail Wren, Bryan Bettesworth, Louise Fisher |
| 1971 | Saskatchewan | Larry McGrath, Darlene Hill, John Gunn, Audrey St. John |
| 1970 | Alberta | Bill Mitchell, Hadie Manley, Bill Tainsh, Connie Reeve |
| 1969 | Alberta | Don Anderson, Bernie Hunter, Bill Tainsh, Connie Reeve |
| 1968 | Saskatchewan | Larry McGrath, Darlene Hill, Peter Gunn, Marlene Dorsett |
| 1967 | Saskatchewan | Larry McGrath, Darlene Hill, Peter Gunn, Marlene Dorsett |
| 1966 | Manitoba | Ernie Boushy, Ina Light, Garry DeBlonde, Betty Hird |
| 1965 | Alberta | Lee Green, Kay Berreth, Shirley Salt, Vi Salt |
| 1964 | Manitoba | Ernie Boushy, Ina Light, Garry DeBlonde, Bea McKenzie |

## The Canadian Senior Men's Champions

| 2002 | Manitoba | Carl German, Ray Fillion, Ray McDougall, Brian Copeland |
| 2001 | Manitoba | Gary Ross, Winston Warren, Gary Smith, Ken Orr |
| 2000 | Ontario | Bob Turcotte, Roy Weigand, Bob Lichti, Steve McDermot |
| 1999 | British Columbia | Ken Watson, Ed Dezura, John Himbury, Howard Grisack |
| 1998 | Saskatchewan | Gary Bryden, Dale Graham, Wilf Foss, Gerry Zimmer |

| 1997 | Ontario | Bob Turcotte, Roy Weigand, Bob Lichti, Steve McDermot |
| 1996 | Ontario | Bob Turcotte, Roy Weigand, Bob Lichti, Steve McDermot |
| 1995 | Ontario | Bill Dickie, Thom Pritchard, Keith MacGregor, George Dolejsi |
| 1994 | New Brunswick | David Sullivan, Wally Nason, Roland Lord, William Ayer |
| 1993 | Alberta | Len Erickson, Merl Brown, Bernie Desjarlais, Nelson Caron |
| 1992 | Ontario | Jim Sharples, Art Lobel, Joe Gurowka, Brian Longley |
| 1991 | Manitoba | Jim Ursel, Norm Houck, John Helston, Stan Lamont |
| 1990 | Manitoba | Jim Ursel, Norm Houck, Stan Lamont, Henry Kroeger |
| 1989 | Ontario | Jim Sharples, Art Lobel, Joe Gurowka, Peter Warren |
| 1988 | Alberta | Bill Clark, Cy Little, Murray MacDonald, John Mayer |
| 1987 | Manitoba | Norm Houck, Henry Kroeger, Sam Doherty, Doug McCartney |
| 1986 | Ontario | Earle Hushagen, Joe Gurowka, Art Lobel, Bert Baragan |
| 1985 | Saskatchewan | Frank Scheirich, Joe Golumbia, Wally Yuzdepski, Alex Wassien |
| 1984 | Manitoba | Lloyd Gunnlaugson, Toru Suzuki, Albert Olson, Elgin Christianson |
| 1983 | Manitoba | Lloyd Gunnlaugson, Toru Suzuki, Albert Olson, Dennis Reid |
| 1982 | Manitoba | Lloyd Gunnlaugson, Toru Suzuki, Albert Olson, Elgin Christianson |
| 1981 | Quebec | Jim Wilson, Garth Ruiter, George Brown, Bert Skitt |
| 1980 | Saskatchewan | Terry McGeary, Don Berglind, Hillis Thompson, Clare Ramsay |
| 1979 | Alberta | Cliff Forry, John Wolfe, Fred Kalicum, Ray Wellman |
| 1978 | Saskatchewan | Art Knutson, Ernie Vaughan, Gay Knutson, Elmer Knutson |
| 1977 | Saskatchewan | Morrie Thompson, Bert Harbottle, Archie Bartley, Mac McKee |
| 1976 | P.E.I. | Wen MacDonald, John Squarebriggs, Irvine MacKinnon, Don Hutchison |
| 1975 | P.E.I. | Wen MacDonald, John Squarebriggs, Irvine MacKinnon, Don Hutchison |
| 1974 | British Columbia | George Beaudry, Buzz McGibney, Tom Clark, Harvey McKay |

| 1973 | Manitoba | Bill McTavish, Bunt McLean, John McLean, Harry Sulkers |
| 1972 | Quebec | Ken Weldon, Ben McCormick, Bob Hubbard, Larry Elliott |
| 1971 | P.E.I. | Wen MacDonald, John Squarebriggs, Doug George, Dan O'Rourke |
| 1970 | British Columbia | Don MacRae, Gene Koster, Bev Smiley, Doc Howden |
| 1969 | Ontario | Alfie Phillips, George Cowan, Sandy McTavish, Jack Young |
| 1968 | Saskatchewan | Don Wilson, Carson Tufts, Ivan McMillan, Reuben Lowe |
| 1967 | New Brunswick | Jim Murphy, Harry Farrell, Don Beatteay, Walter Biddiscombe |
| 1966 | Ontario | Jim Johnston, Tom Rosborough, Joe Todd, Ed Waller |
| 1965 | Manitoba | Leo Johnson, Marno Frederickson, Fred Smith, Cliff Wise |

## The Canadian Senior Women's Champions

| 2002 | Ontario | Anne Dunn, Lindy Marchuk, Gloria Campbell, Carol Thompson |
| 2001 | Ontario | Anne Dunn, Lindy Marchuk, Gloria Campbell, Fran Todd |
| 2000 | Quebec | Agnès Charette, Martha Don, Lois Baines, Mary Anne Robertson |
| 1999 | Quebec | Agnès Charette, Martha Don, Lois Baines, Mary Anne Robertson |
| 1998 | Ontario | Jill Greenwood, Yvonne Smith, Gloria Campbell, Vicki Lauder |
| 1997 | Quebec | Agnès Charette, Martha Don, Lois Baines, Mary Anne Robertson |
| 1996 | Ontario | Jill Greenwood, Yvonne Smith, Gloria Campbell, Vicki Lauder |
| 1995 | Northern Ontario | Sheila Ross, Linda Anderson, Barbara Gordon, Rae D'Agostino |
| 1994 | Alberta | Cordella Schwengler, Marj Stewart, Betty Clarke, Nora Eaves |
| 1993 | Ontario | Jill Greenwood, Yvonne Smith, Vicki Lauder, Maymar Gemmell |
| 1992 | Saskatchewan | Sheila Rowan, Donna Trapp, Doreen Thomas, Joyce McKee |
| 1991 | Northern Ontario | Eila Brown, Arline Wilson, Eileen Chivers-Wilson, Betty Toskovich |

| 1990 | Ontario | Jill Greenwood, Yvonne Smith, Maymar Gemmell, Vicki Lauder |
|------|---------|-----|
| 1989 | Saskatchewan | Emily Farnham, Mary Todarchuk, Mary Heidt, Arlie Ellsworth |
| 1988 | Ontario | Phyllis Nielsen, Barbara Baird, Geraldine Barton, Mary Ellen McGugan |
| 1987 | Nova Scotia | Verda Kempton, Marita Morrow, Joan Mason, Molly Pirie |
| 1986 | Saskatchewan | Ev Krahn, Twyla Widdifield, Shirley Little, June Kaufman |
| 1985 | Saskatchewan | Ev Krahn, Twyla Widdifield, Shirley Little, June Kaufman |
| 1984 | Saskatchewan | Ev Krahn, Twyla Widdifield, Shirley Little, June Kaufman |
| 1983 | Manitoba | Mabel Mitchell, Mary Adams, Mildred Murray, June Clark |
| 1982 | Nova Scotia | Verda Kempton, Lucille Hamm, Molly Pirie, Lois Smith |
| 1981 | Alberta | Bea Mayer, Eileen Cyr, Leah Nate, Alice Vejprava |
| 1980 | British Columbia | Flora Martin, Elsie Humphrey, Verle McKeown, Edna Messum |
| 1979 | British Columbia | Flora Martin, Elsie Humphrey, Verle McKeown, Edna Messum |
| 1978 | Alberta | Hadie Manley, Bernie Durward, Dee McIntyre, Anna Kasting |
| 1977 | British Columbia | Vi Tapella, Rose Neratini, Doris Driesche, Mary Lee Bacchus |
| 1976 | Alberta | Hadie Manley, Bernie Durward, Anna Kasting, Gladys Baptist |
| 1975 | British Columbia | Flora Martin, Edna Messum, Doreen Baker, Betty Stubbs |
| 1974 | British Columbia | Flora Martin, Edna Messum, Doreen Baker, Betty Stubbs |
| 1973 | British Columbia | Ada Calles, Ina Hansen, May Shaw, Barbara Weir |

## The World Men's Champions

| 2002 | Canada | Randy Ferbey, David Nedohin, Scott Pfeifer, Marcel Rocque |
|------|--------|-----|
| 2001 | Sweden | Peter Lindholm, Tomas Nordin, Magnus Swartling, Peter Narup |
| 2000 | Canada | Greg McAulay, Brent Pierce, Bryan Miki, Jody Sveistrup |
| 1999 | Scotland | Hammy McMillan, Warwick Smith, Ewan MacDonald, Peter Loudon |

| 1998 | Canada | Wayne Middaugh, Graeme McCarrel, Ian Tetley, Scott Bailey |
|------|--------|----------------------------------------------------------|
| 1997 | Sweden | Peter Lindholm, Tomas Nordin, Magnus Swartling, Peter Narup |
| 1996 | Canada | Jeff Stoughton, Ken Tresoor, Garry Vandenberghe, Steve Gould |
| 1995 | Canada | Kerry Burtnyk, Jeff Ryan, Rob Meakin, Keith Fenton |
| 1994 | Canada | Rick Folk, Pat Ryan, Bert Gretzinger, Gerry Richard |
| 1993 | Canada | Russ Howard, Glenn Howard, Wayne Middaugh, Peter Corner |
| 1992 | Switzerland | Markus Eggler, Frederic Jean, Stefan Hofer, Bjorn Schroder |
| 1991 | Scotland | David Smith, Graeme Connal, Peter Smith, David Hay |
| 1990 | Canada | Ed Werenich, John Kawaja, Ian Tetley, Pat Perroud |
| 1989 | Canada | Pat Ryan, Randy Ferbey, Don Walchuk, Don McKenzie |
| 1988 | Norway | Eigil Ramsfjell, Sjur Loen, Morten Sogaard, Bo Bakke |
| 1987 | Canada | Russ Howard, Glenn Howard, Tim Belcourt, Kent Carstairs |
| 1986 | Canada | Ed Lukowich, John Ferguson, Neil Houston, Brent Syme |
| 1985 | Canada | Al Hackner, Rick Lang, Ian Tetley, Pat Perroud |
| 1984 | Norway | Eigil Ramsfjell, Sjur Loen, Gunnar Meland, Bo Bakke |
| 1983 | Canada | Ed Werenich, Paul Savage, John Kawaja, Neil Harrison |
| 1982 | Canada | Al Hackner, Rick Lang, Bob Nicol, Bruce Kennedy |
| 1981 | Switzerland | Jurg Tanner, Jurg Hornisberger, Patrick Loertscher, Franz Tanner |
| 1980 | Canada | Rick Folk, Ron Mills, Tom Wilson, Jim Wilson |
| 1979 | Norway | Kristian Soerum, Morten Soerum, Eigil Ramsfjell, Gunnar Meland |
| 1978 | United States | Bob Nichols, Bill Strum, Tom Locken, Bob Christman |
| 1977 | Sweden | Ragnar Kamp, Hakan Rudstrom, Bjorn Rudstrom, Christer Martensson |
| 1976 | United States | Bruce Roberts, Joe Roberts, Gary Kleffman, Jerry Scott |
| 1975 | Switzerland | Otto Danieli, Roland Schneider, Rolf Gautschi, Ueli Mulli |
| 1974 | United States | Bud Somerville, Bob Nichols, Bill Strum, Tom Locken |
| 1973 | Sweden | Kjell Oscarius, Bengt Oscarius, Tom Schaeffer, Boa Carlman |
| 1972 | Canada | Orest Meleschuk, Dave Romano, John Hanesiak, Pat Hailley |

| 1971 | Canada | Don Duguid, Rod Hunter, Jim Pettapiece, Bryan Wood |
| 1970 | Canada | Don Duguid, Rod Hunter, Jim Pettapiece, Bryan Wood |
| 1969 | Canada | Ron Northcott, Dave Gerlach, Bernie Sparkes, Fred Storey |
| 1968 | Canada | Ron Northcott, Jimmy Shields, Bernie Sparkes, Fred Storey |
| 1967 | Scotland | Chuck Hay, John Bryden, Alan Glen, David Howie |
| 1966 | Canada | Ron Northcott, George Fink, Bernie Sparkes, Fred Storey |
| 1965 | United States | Bud Somerville, Bill Strum, Al Gagne, Tom Wright |
| 1964 | Canada | Lyall Dagg, Leo Hebert, Fred Britton, Barry Naimark |
| 1963 | Canada | Ernie Richardson, Arnold Richardson, Garnet Richardson, Mel Perry |
| 1962 | Canada | Ernie Richardson, Arnold Richardson, Garnet Richardson, Wes Richardson |
| 1961 | Canada | Hector Gervais, Ray Werner, Vic Raymer, Wally Ursuliak |
| 1960 | Canada | Ernie Richardson, Arnold Richardson, Garnet Richardson, Wes Richardson |
| 1959 | Canada | Ernie Richardson, Arnold Richardson, Garnet Richardson, Wes Richardson |

## The World Women's Champions

| 2002 | Scotland | Jackie Lockhart, Sheila Swan, Katriona Fairweather, Ann Laird |
| 2001 | Canada | Colleen Jones, Kim Kelly, Mary-Anne Waye, Nancy Delahunt |
| 2000 | Canada | Kelley Law, Julie Skinner, Georgina Wheatcroft, Diane Nelson |
| 1999 | Sweden | Elisabet Gustafson, Katarina Nyberg, Lousie Marmont, Elisabeth Persson |
| 1998 | Sweden | Elisabet Gustafson, Katarina Nyberg, Louise Marmont, Elisabeth Persson |
| 1997 | Canada | Sandra Schmirler, Jan Betker, Joan McCusker, Marcia Gudereit |
| 1996 | Canada | Marilyn Bodogh, Kim Gellard, Corie Beveridge, Jane Hooper Perroud |
| 1995 | Sweden | Elisabet Gustafson, Katarina Nyberg, Louise Marmont, Elisabeth Persson |

| 1994 | Canada | Sandra Schmirler, Jan Betker, Joan McCusker, Marcia Gudereit |
|------|--------|---|
| 1993 | Canada | Sandra Schmirler, Jan Betker, Joan McCusker, Marcia Gudereit |
| 1992 | Sweden | Elisabet Gustafson, Katarina Nyberg, Louise Marmont, Elisabeth Persson |
| 1991 | Norway | Dordi Nordby, Hanne Pettersen, Mette Halvorsen, Anne Jotun |
| 1990 | Norway | Dordi Nordby, Hanne Pettersen, Mette Halvorsen, Anne Jotun |
| 1989 | Canada | Heather Houston, Lorraine Lang, Diane Adams, Tracy Kennedy |
| 1988 | Germany | Andrea Schöpp, Almut Scholl, Monika Wagner, Suzanne Fink |
| 1987 | Canada | Pat Sanders, Georgina Hawkes, Louise Herlinveaux, Deb Massullo |
| 1986 | Canada | Marilyn Bodogh, Kathy McEdwards, Chris Jurgenson, Jan Augustyn |
| 1985 | Canada | Linda Moore, Lindsay Sparkes, Debbie Jones, Laurie Carney |
| 1984 | Canada | Connie Laliberte, Chris More, Corinne Peters, Janet Arnott |
| 1983 | Switzerland | Erika Müller, Barbara Meyer, Barbara Meier, Christina Wirz |
| 1982 | Denmark | Marianne Jorgenson, Helena Blach, Astrid Birnbaum, Jette Olsen |
| 1981 | Sweden | Elisabeth Hogstrom, Carina Olsson, Birgitta Sewick, Karin Sjogran |
| 1980 | Canada | Marj Mitchell, Nancy Kerr, Shirley McKendry, Wendy Leach |
| 1979 | Switzerland | Gaby Casanova, Rosie Manger, Linda Thommen, Betty Bourguin |

## The World Junior Men's Champions

| 2002 | Canada | David Hamblin, Ross Derksen, Kevin Hamblin, Ross McCannell |
|------|--------|---|
| 2001 | Canada | Brad Gushue, Mark Nichols, Brent Hamilton, Mike Adam |
| 2000 | Canada | Brad Kuhn, Kevin Folk, Ryan Kuhn, Hugh Bennett |

| | | |
|------|---------------|---------------------------------------------------------------------|
| 1999 | Canada | John Morris, Craig Savill, Jason Young, Brent Laing |
| 1998 | Canada | John Morris, Craig Savill, Andy Ormsby, Brent Laing |
| 1997 | Switzerland | Ralph Stöckli, Michael Boesiger, Pascal Sieber, Clemens Oberwiler |
| 1996 | Scotland | James Dryburgh, Ross Barnet, Ron Brewster, David Murdoch |
| 1995 | Scotland | Tom Brewster, Paul Westwood, Ronald Brewster, Steven Still |
| 1994 | Canada | Colin Davison, Kelly Mittelstadt, Scott Pfeifer, Sean Morris |
| 1993 | Scotland | Craig Wilson, Neil Murdoch, Ricky Burnett, Craig Strawhorn |
| 1992 | Switzerland | Stefan Heilmann, Christoph Grossenbacher, Lucian Jenzer, Roger Wyss |
| 1991 | Scotland | Alan MacDougall, James Dryburgh, Fraser MacGregor, Colin Beckett |
| 1990 | Switzerland | Stefan Traub, Andreas Oestreich, Markus Widmer, Roland Muessler |
| 1989 | Sweden | Peter Lindholm, Magnus Swartling, Owe Ljundahl, Peter Narup |
| 1988 | Canada | Jim Sullivan, Charles Sullivan, Craig Burgess, Dan Alderman |
| 1987 | Scotland | Douglas Dryburgh, Philip Wilson, Lindsay Clark, Billy Andrew |
| 1986 | Scotland | David Aitken, Robin Halliday, Peter Smith, Harry Reilly |
| 1985 | Canada | Bob Ursel, Brent Mendella, Gerald Chick, Mike Ursel |
| 1984 | United States | Al Edwards, Mark Larson, Dewey Basley, Kurt Disher |
| 1983 | Canada | John Base, Bruce Webster, Dave McAnerney, Jim Donahoe |
| 1982 | Sweden | Soren Grahn, Niklas Jarund, Henrik Holmberg, Anders Vennerstedt |
| 1981 | Scotland | Peter Wilson, Jim Cannon, Roger McIntyre, John Parker |
| 1980 | Scotland | Andrew McQuistin, Norman Brown, Hugh Aitken, Dick Adams |
| 1979 | United States | Don Barcome, Randy Darling, Bobby Stalker, Earl Barcome |
| 1978 | Canada | Paul Gowsell, John Ferguson, Doug MacFarlane, Kelly Stearne |
| 1977 | Canada | Bill Jenkins, John Scales, Sandy Stewart, Alan Mayhew |

| 1976 | Canada | Paul Gowsell, Neil Houston, Glen Jackson, Kelly Stearne |
| 1975 | Sweden | Jan Ullsten, Mats Nyberg, Anders Grahn, Bo Soderstrom |

## The World Junior Women's Champions

| 2002 | United States | Cassandra Johnson, Jamie Johnson, Katie Beck, Maureen Brunt |
| 2001 | Canada | Suzanne Gaudet, Stefanie Richard, Robyn MacPhee, Kelly Higgins |
| 2000 | Sweden | Matilda Mattsson, Kajsa Bergström, Lisa Löfskog, Jenny Hammarström |
| 1999 | Switzerland | Silvana Tirinzoni, Michèle Knobel, Brigitte Schori, Martina von Arx |
| 1998 | Canada | Melissa McClure, Nancy Toner, Brigitte McClure, Bethany Toner |
| 1997 | Scotland | Julia Ewart, Michelle Silvera, Mhairi Ferguson, Lynn Cameron |
| 1996 | Canada | Heather Godberson, Carmen Whyte, Kristie Moore, Terelyn Bloor |
| 1995 | Canada | Kelly MacKenzie, Joanne Fillion, Carlene Muth, Sasha Bergner |
| 1994 | Canada | Kim Gellard, Corie Beveridge, Lisa Savage, Sandy Graham |
| 1993 | Scotland | Kirsty Hay, Gillian Barr, Joanna Pegg, Louise Wilkie |
| 1992 | Scotland | Gillian Barr, Claire Milne, Janice Watt, Nikki Mauchline |
| 1991 | Sweden | Eva Eriksson, Maria Soderkvist, Asa Eriksson, Elisabeth de Brito |
| 1990 | Scotland | Kirsty Addison, Karen Addison, Joanna Pegg, Laura Scott |
| 1989 | Canada | LaDawn Funk, Sandy Symyrozum, Cindy Larsen, Laurelle Funk |
| 1988 | Canada | Julie Sutton, Judy Wood, Susan Auty, Marla Geiger |

## The World Senior Men's Champions

| 2002 | USA | Larry Johnston, Stan Vinge, George Godfrey, Bill Kidd, Steve Brown |

### The World Senior Women's Champions

| 2002 | Canada | Anne Dunn, Lindy Marchuk, Gloria Campbell, Carol Thompson, Fran Todd |
|------|--------|-----------------------------------------------------------------------|

### World Wheelchair Champions

| 2002 | Switzerland | Urs Bucher, Cesare Cassani, Manfred Bolllinger, Therese Kämpfer, Silvia Obrist |
|------|-------------|---------------------------------------------------------------------------------|

### World Curling Freytag Award Winners

| 2002 | Switzerland | Franz Tanner |
|------|-------------|--------------|
| 2001 | USA | Bud Somerville (curler) |
| | Canada | Shirley Morash (builder) |
| 2000 | Canada | Ernie Richardson (curler) |
| | USA | Bob Hardy (builder) |
| 1999 | | not awarded |
| 1998 | | not awarded |
| 1997 | Switzerland | Erwin Sautter |
| 1996 | Scotland | Elizabeth Paterson-Brown |
| 1995 | | not awarded |
| 1994 | Germany | Keith Wendorf |
| 1993 | | not awarded |
| 1992 | | not awarded |
| 1991 | | not awarded |
| 1990 | Canada | Colin Campbell |
| 1989 | | not awarded |

### Elmer Freytag Memorial Award Winners

| 1988 | USA | Kay Sugahara |
|------|-----|--------------|
| 1987 | Canada | Bob Picken |
| 1986 | USA | Art Cobb |
| 1985 | Canada | Don McLeod |
| 1984 | Scotland | Robin Welsh |

| 1983 | Canada | Mabel DeWare |
| 1982 | Sweden | Sven Eklund |
| 1981 | Canada | Doug Maxwell |
| 1980 | Scotland | Bob Grierson |
| 1979 | Scotland | Chuck Hay |
| 1978 | Canada | Ken Watson |

## Colin Campbell Memorial Award Winners

| 2002 | Norway | Pål Trulsen |
| 2001 | France | Spencer Mugnier |
| 2000 | Canada | Greg McAulay |
| 1999 | New Zealand | Sean Becker |
| 1998 | Finland | Markku Uusipaavalniemi |
| 1997 | Finland | Jussi Uusipaavalniemi |
| 1996 | Sweden | Mikael Hasselborg |
| 1995 | Sweden | Peter Lindholm |
| 1994 | Denmark | Gert Larsen |
| 1993 | Australia | Hugh Millikin |
| 1992 | Finland | Jussi Uusipaavalniemi |
| 1991 | Switzerland | Markus Eggler |
| 1990 | Denmark | Tommy Stjerne |
| 1989 | Denmark | Tommy Stjerne |
| 1988 | Norway | Bo Bakke |
| 1987 | Sweden | Goran Roxin |
| 1986 | Germany | Uli Sutor |
| 1985 | USA | Tim Wright |
| 1984 | Scotland | Mike Hay |
| 1983 | Germany | Keith Wendorf |
| 1982 | Canada | Rick Lang |
| 1981 | Canada | Mark Olson |
| 1980 | Scotland | Greig Henderson |
| 1979 | Germany | Keith Wendorf |

**Frances Brodie Award Winners**

| 2002 | Korea | Mi-Yeon Kim |
|------|-------|-------------|
| 2001 | USA | Ann Swisshelm |
| 2000 | Scotland | Rhona Martin |
| 1999 | Norway | Marianne Aspelin |
| 1998 | Scotland | Jackie Lockhart |
| 1997 | Finland | Jaana Jokela |
| 1996 | Scotland | Kirsty Hay |
| 1995 | Japan | Ayako Ishigaki |
| 1994 | Denmark | Helena Blach-Lavrsen |
| 1993 | Finland | Jaana Jokela |
| 1992 | USA | Amy Hatten Wright |
| 1991 | Austria | Veronika Huber |
| 1990 | Germany | Almut Hege-Scholl |
| 1989 | Switzerland | Cristina Lestander |

# A Glossary of Abbreviations

CCA      Canadian Curling Association (successor to the DCA)

CCN      *Canadian Curling News*

CLCA      Canadian Ladies' Curling Association

DCA      Dominion Curling Association

FGZ      Free Guard Zone

GCCC      Grand Caledonian Curling Club (later to become the RCCC)

ICF      International Curling Federation (later to become the WCF)

IOC      International Olympic Committee

LWCC      Ladies' World Curling Championship

OCA      Ontario Curling Association

RCCC      Royal Caledonian Curling Club

USCA      United States Curling Association

WCC      World Curling Championship(s)

WCF      World Curling Federation

WCPA      World Curling Players' Association

WCT      World Curling Tour

WJCC      World Junior Curling Championships

WLCC      World Ladies' Curling Championship

WWCC      World Women's Curling Championship

# Bibliography

Argan, William. *Saskatchewan Curling—Heartland Tradition.* Regina: Saskatchewan Curling Association, 1991.

Arnup, John D. *The Toronto Curling Club 1836–1957.* Toronto: Toronto Cricket, Skating and Curling Club, 1984.

Bicket, James. *The Canadian Curlers Manual.* Toronto: Office of the British Colonist, Hugh Scobie—Printer, 1840.

Boreham, H. Bruce. *The Brier—Canada's Curling Classic 1927–1969.* Published privately, 1954.

Bryden, Wendy. *Canada at the Olympic Winter Games.* Edmonton: Hurtig Publishers, 1987.

Calgary Curling Club. *A Roaring Century 1888–1988.* Calgary: Calgary Curling Club, 1988.

Cowan, Bob. *Curling and the Silver Broom.* Glasgow: Richard Drew Publishing, 1985.

Creelman, W. A. *Curling Past and Present.* Toronto: McClelland & Stewart Limited, 1950.

Curl BC. *The History of Curling in British Columbia.* Vancouver: Curl BC, 1995.

Dowbiggin, Bruce. *The Stick.* Toronto: Macfarlane Walter and Ross, 2001.

Fillmore, Stanley. *The Pleasure of the Game: The Story of the Toronto Cricket, Skating and Curling Club 1827–1977*. Toronto: Hunter Rose Company Ltd., 1977.

Garcelon, Alan, ed. *New Brunswick Curling Records 1854–1993*. Fredericton: New Brunswick Curling Association, 1933.

Girouard, Mark. *The Return to Camelot, Chivalry and the English Gentleman*. New Haven, CT/London, UK: Yale University Press, 1981.

Gray, James H. *The Roar of the Twenties*. Toronto: Macmillan Company of Canada, 1975.

Gray, James H. *The Winter Years*. Toronto: Macmillan Company of Canada, 1966.

Harper, Col. J. R., OBE, TD. *78th Fighting Frasers 1757–1763*. Chomedy, Laval, PQ: DEV-SCO Publications Ltd., 1966.

Harper, J. R. *The Fraser Highlanders*. 2nd ed. Bloomfield, ON: for the David M. Stewart Museum by Museum Restoration Service, 1995.

Howell, Nancy, and Maxwell Howell. *Sport and Games in Canadian Life, 1700 to the Present*. Toronto: Macmillan Company of Canada, 1969.

Jenkyns, Richard. *Dignity and Decadence, Victorian Art and the Classical Inheritance*. Toronto: HarperCollins Publishers, 1991.

Kerr, Rev. John. *Curling in Canada and the USA: A record of the tour of the Scottish team, 1902–03, and of the game in the Dominion and the Republic*. Edinburgh: Geo. A. Morton, 1904.

Lefko, Perry. *Sandra Schmirler, Queen of Curling*. Toronto: Stoddart Publishing Company Ltd., 2000.

Ludwig, Jack. *Games of Fear and Winning*. Toronto: Doubleday Canada Ltd., 1976.

Lukowich, Ed, Al Hackner, and Rick Lang. *Curling to Win*. Toronto: McGraw-Hill Ryerson Limited, 1986.

Lukowich, Ed, Eigil Ramsfjell, and Bud Somerville. *The Joy of Curling, a Celebration*. Toronto: McGraw-Hill Ryerson, 1990.

Maxwell, Doug, Ernie Richardson, and Joyce McKee. *Curling*. Toronto: Thos. Allen Ltd., 1962.

Maxwell, Doug, and friends. *The First Fifty.* Toronto: Maxcurl Publications, 1980.

Murray, W. H. *The Curling Companion.* Rev. ed. Don Mills, ON: Collins Publishers, 1981.

Nelson, Emery. *One Hundred and Fifty Years of Curling, 1834–1984.* Fergus, ON: The Fergus Curling Club and Fergus Instant Print, 1983.

Proulx, Rita. *The Squealing Circles.* Quebec City: self-published, 2000.

*The Royal Montreal Curling Club.* Montreal: Royal Montreal Curling Club, 1932. (Published by the club on the occasion of its 125th anniversary in 1932.)

Sautter, Erwin A. *Curling-Vademecum.* Printed in Switzerland, 1993.

Savage, Paul. *Curling: Hack to House.* Markham, ON: Paper Jacks Ltd., 1983.

Scholz, Guy. *Gold on Ice: The Story of the Sandra Schmirler Curling Team.* Regina: Coteau Books, 1999.

Schrodt, Barbara, Gerald Redmond, and Richard Baka. *Sport Canadiana.* Edmonton: Executive Sport Publications Ltd., 1980.

Smith, David B. *Curling: an Illustrated History.* Edinburgh: John Donald Publishers Ltd., 1981.

Sonmor, Jean. *Burned by the Rock.* Toronto: Macmillan Canada, 1991.

Stevenson, John A. *Curling in Ontario 1846–1946.* Toronto: Ontario Curling Association and The Ryerson Press, 1950.

Tiefenbach, Arnie. *Say It Again, Sam!* Regina: The House That Sam Built & Future Marketing, 1999.

Traill, Catharine Parr. *The Backwoods of Canada.* Toronto: McClelland & Stewart, 1929.

Triggs, Stanley G. *The Stamp of a Studio.* Toronto: Coach House Press, 1985.

Watson, Ken. *Ken Watson On Curling.* Toronto: Copp Clark Publishing Company, 1950.

Weeks, Bob. *The Brier. The History of Canada's Most Celebrated Curling Championship.* Toronto: Macmillan Canada, 1995.

Welsh, Robin. *Beginner's Guide to Curling.* London, UK: Pelham Books Ltd., 1969.

# Index

*Numbers in italic refer to captions.*